Writing and Selling
Fillers and Short Humor

Writing and Selling
Fillers and Short Humor

Edited by
A. S. BURACK

Publishers   THE WRITER, INC.   *Boston*

PREFACE

This book has been prepared to help you write and sell fillers and short humor. The various chapters have been written by authors and editors who generously share with you their long experience in this field, and provide entertaining, instructive examples of successful short features.

Also included are the simple rules you should know about preparing and submitting manuscripts, plus a comprehensive market list with the names and addresses of publications which purchase short items. Full information on what editors are looking for and what they will buy follows each listing.

The response of the authors and editors who contributed instruction and market information to this book has been most enthusiastic—and I am sure you will match their enthusiasm as you discover the pleasure and profit to be derived from this wide-open field.

A. S. BURACK

BOSTON, MASS.

CONTENTS

PART I

Editor of The Writer *magazine for more than twenty years,* A. S. BURACK *has had long experience with authors and authorship.* He has been an instructor at Boston University and a guest lecturer at many writers' conferences, including Tufts University and The University of New Hampshire. He is the editor of several textbooks on writing technique, among them *The Writer's Handbook,* The Craft of Novel Writing, *and* Writing Detective and Mystery Fiction.

I

WRITING FILLERS AND SHORT ITEMS

BY A. S. BURACK

The fillers and short items that liven up the pages of hundreds of magazines today are becoming increasingly important to editors. Originally inserted to fill end-of-the-column and bottom-of-the-page spaces, they are now featured parts of most magazines. Many readers search out these informative and entertaining items first—skimming through the whole issue from cover to cover to find them —before they start reading the longer stories or articles.

Opportunities for writers in this field are most attractive, especially for beginners. You don't need a famous name to sell a joke, a two-line filler, a recipe or an anecdote. If you can supply editors with the kind of fillers and short humor they want, they will buy from you even if you've never before written a single word for publication.

The time you devote to this field of writing may range from a full daily schedule to a part-time hobby—or just an occasional try at breaking into print with a quip, verse, or other brief item. It's the kind of writing that can be done at any time and in almost any place. You can keep regular working hours at your desk, or you can fit your planning and writing in among your usual everyday activities. A considerable amount of writing can be done while you are commuting to work, doing household chores, eating lunch, or even when you are convalescing from an illness. There is hardly a time during the day when you cannot collect ideas for publishable short items. Listen to the quips or amusing anecdotes related by your co-workers. Train yourself to "hear" the bright sayings of children. Watch for the unusual or helpful solution to a problem. Make mental notes of these—and then get them down on paper at the first opportunity.

Your reading, too, can be productive. Look for clever phrases, humorous errors in print, interesting or little-known facts—all these can bring you dividends. And remember, also, that although new and original ideas are always needed and wanted by editors, no subject, no matter how commonplace, should be ignored as possible filler material. For example, many a new bride doesn't know the proper way to scramble an egg. There are new brides every day, and a simple restatement of how to make good scrambled eggs may bring you a check. Every December, magazines want to remind Christmas tree owners of certain fire prevention rules; a brief list of these, properly written up, is bound to find a market. Each spring, some magazine will tell its readers how to recognize and treat poison ivy; next year, it could be *your* little article on this subject that will appear in print.

There are innumerable markets for short items of every variety, and the payment ranges from pin-money to substantial sums. *Look Magazine* pays $10.00 for a one-line epigram. Good anecdotes about doctors may bring $25.00 to $40.00 from *Medical Economics*. A handy man can get $12.00 from *Popular Mechanics* for short fact items about tools or shop hints. *The New Yorker* pays $5.00 and up for "newsbreaks," amusing typographical errors or misprints, stilted or exaggerated expressions, etc. Housewives may receive from $3.00 to $6.00 from *Woman's Day* for practical suggestions, household and child care hints, etc. *Playboy* pays $25 to $200 for brief amusing paragraphs on topical subjects. *The Reader's Digest* pays up to $100.00 for a wide variety of material, including "Toward a More Picturesque Speech," "Quotable Quotes," "Life in These United States," etc.

Practically everything you do is a possible source of ideas for short items. Cleaning a closet may give you ideas for a humorous paragraph or two—or perhaps you'll be able to write up an efficient way of dealing with this chore. If you've given or attended a successful party recently, remember that novel party ideas are always in demand— special decorations for children's parties, menus and games for teen-agers, shower ideas, etc. Do you have any gardening tricks? Many magazines are interested in them. Have you made a lamp from some unusual materials? Helpful decorating features will almost always find a market. Hints on child-rearing can bring many small checks. How do you handle the problem of traveling with children? This could be the subject of a helpful article or it could be written up humorously. Have you worked out a clever merchandising scheme for your business? Do you have a short cut that has proved helpful in your job? There are trade and business publications for almost every business or profession, and these may welcome write-ups of such ideas.

Writing short items requires no special training. Editors are primarily interested in helpful information they can pass on to their readers. Ideas should be set down clearly and simply. Keep in mind that the style used in most fillers—from short fact articles to one-line hints—is informal, conversational.

When you write up an article for publication, pretend that you are sharing an idea, a hint or a story with someone you know. The friendly approach brings good results.

Here are a few basic points to keep in mind when writing up an idea:

1) First and foremost, ask yourself, "Do I have a solution to a problem?" The "problem" may be something as simple as what to feed hungry children when they come home from school, but your item should offer a real solution to a common problem. And, speaking of common problems, your next question should be, "Do people who read this publication have this problem, so that the editor will feel it belongs in his pages?"

2) Next, consider the appeal of your idea. Will it be interesting and helpful to readers? If you want to submit some recipes, ask yourself if they are easy to prepare, nutritious and economical. Would the dishes have eye-appeal; do they tempt fussy appetites? Also, have you checked your recipe carefully? Be sure ingredients and timing are correct when you submit recipes—your dishes must turn out right in the magazines' test kitchens.

3) How-to-do-it pieces must also be precise and detailed. Have you made your directions simple enough for any amateur to follow? Are all of the measurements accurate in your description of how to build a coffee table from scrap

lumber? It's best to give step-by-step instructions—either number your directions or say, "First, prepare this. Then, do that, etc." Always suggest substitutes for material or equipment that may not be available in some areas. This is particularly important to magazines with national circulations.

4) One last point: timeliness. While editorial schedules and needs differ, chances are that an editor will not be buying hints for Christmas decorations in November; at that time his Christmas issue is already being printed or is on the newsstands, and few editors like to save material for a whole year. Therefore, holiday, special occasion or seasonal material should usually be submitted to monthly magazines from four to seven months in advance, and eight or ten weeks ahead to weekly publications.

You may not be able to decide immediately what form your idea should take—should it be written up as a brief hint, or should you expand it to a short feature? Should you give it humorous or serious treatment? This will often depend upon your own experience and temperament. If something strikes you funny, perhaps you should try the humorous approach; if it's the *information* that mainly interests you, write it up factually. Sometimes it's best to gather several related ideas and present them as a brief feature built around a central theme.

When you send accompanying diagrams or photographs, be sure these are as clear as possible. In case your own photographs do not turn out well, it will be worth your while to arrange for a competent amateur to take the picture. Payment arrangements for this vary, but most of the time you can pay the photographer a certain percentage of your check. Moreover, you'll find that many magazines pay extra for photographs.

In this "read-as-you-run" age, fillers, quips, anecdotes, etc. will receive careful reading in the editorial offices of hundreds of publications. Editors always need fresh sources of supply to keep their stock of material varied and up-to-date. *Your* brief contributions may find a ready welcome in their pages.

PARKE CUMMINGS *has contributed short humor items to* The Saturday Evening Post, Look, Maclean's, Family Weekly, 1,000 Jokes, *and several other magazines. His longer humor pieces have appeared in* Redbook, Coronet, Pageant, The Lion *and* The Rotarian. *Mr. Cummings' serious writing covers the world of sports. In this line, he has written for* The New Yorker *and the* Encyclopedia Americana *and is the author of a book,* American Tennis, *a history of the sport in the United States.*

II

SHORT PROSE HUMOR

BY PARKE CUMMINGS

In discussing our subject, we humorists tend to develop a sort of defense complex, a reluctance to bill ourselves as "authorities." This is because humor is as hard to define as "beauty," "wisdom," or "good"—and if you point out that defining these is not only difficult but downright impossible (as far as suiting everybody), I won't argue. In the case of humor, editors make this abundantly clear to us. If you want to sell a long factual article on, let us say, atomic submarines, you submit the idea to an editor first. If you can convince him that you have some fresh and interesting material and that you are a capable writer, you have a chance of getting the assignment.

But mention an idea for a humorous piece to an editor, particularly a short one (very generally, here I am discuss-

17

ing material from 100 to 500 words), and what does he say? He *may* say, "Doesn't appeal to me," or "It's been done before." In that case you may be luckier than you suspect. Because, on the other hand, he may remark, "Sounds like a pretty good idea." This would be fine, and very encouraging, if he stopped there. He never does. I will bet that every humorist in the country could stand up and recite in unison his next ten words: ". . . But of course it all depends on how it's handled." Press him on how it *should* be handled, and he will say either, "That's up to you, naturally," or "Handle it so it's funny."

All very well, but it doesn't help much. Understand, though, that I'm not blaming the editor. He realizes how elusive the subject is. Often he makes the point in another way: "Something might double me up and leave the next guy cold." (Or he will put it the other way around.) In many magazines, more than one editor passes on the material. I have had rejects with comments like, "I liked this a lot, but it didn't get the necessary votes." Occasionally this has worked in reverse—or I've suspected that it did. I've had an acceptance with a rather lukewarm comment, as if to imply that this particular editor thought poorly of it but was overruled by the chuckle-headed majority.

For these reasons, I usually send material in "cold," without first submitting the idea. The exception is an occasional longer piece where I feel that the subject matter is so good that it would be virtually impossible for me to louse it up. But I am discussing shorts, and with these an additional reason is that in a very short piece, I could probably use up more time—and more words—outlining the idea than I would in writing the actual piece.

My next policy—I observe it 99% of the time—is not to grumble (audibly, at any rate) when something is turned down. The only general exception I make is in the case, previously mentioned, where an editor returns a piece that he liked but was overruled on. Here I may comment, in my next letter, "Yeah—I agree; they let a good one get away." I don't really think this has any effect on the editor in question, but it makes *me* feel better.

Further advice I would submit to a writer of short humor is: Be prepared for a certain number of rejections. Maybe the genius doesn't get them, but I am not a genius, and I don't think my advice would be of much value to writers who *are*. We constantly hear that there is a large demand for humor, but there are also a great many writers submitting it. The short variety I speak of rarely takes up more than a page in a magazine. Cartoons may occupy half of that space, and verse and quips often get their share.

My feeling is that I am operating in a rather crowded profession. I think *most* of the material I submit is good —that little of it is actually bad—but the hitch is that it must be *very* good to win out over the material from competitors. And, if you happen to hit a good streak with a certain magazine, you may possibly become your own competitor. The editor of that magazine has so much of your accepted material on hand, and not yet printed, that he hesitates to buy more. Let me hastily add that my troubles on that score have been few and far between.

I suppose most of the above sounds discouraging. Well, I'll stick to my guns and insist that I've found it a tough, competitive field with many disappointments. But there are things to be said in its favor. I feel that a newcomer has a better chance of breaking into this field of writing than into many others. If he *does* have the stuff—the knack of being funny that I cannot define—it doesn't take years of apprenticeship. Let him get a fresh idea, and he may even sell the first piece he submits.

Funny ideas come from every conceivable source. A practicing lawyer, for instance, might get a salable, amusing idea not only about some phase of the law, but also about small boys, outboard motorboats, demagogic politicians, outdoor grille parties, skiing, P.T.A. meetings, space satellites—anything that has come into his realm of experience. If he gets the magic slant that tickles other people's funnybones, he is in.

For this reason, there are some people with steady jobs of all varieties who write short humor on the side. I don't want to give the impression that this can be done with the left foot. My point is simply that a busy housewife or a man with a nine-to-five office job has a better chance of turning out an acceptable short humor piece than of turning out a successful three-act play or a 600-page novel. Probably the latter feats have been accomplished, but I'd say they were considerably rarer.

By and large, humor pay is good. For the time I've put into certain pieces, I feel I've been very well rewarded— remembering, of course, that the average pay goes down considerably when you add in the time spent on the ones that didn't sell. It points up the fact that there probably *is* a large demand for humor.

And there's a personal satisfaction, too. I've pointed out that people differ widely on what they think is funny. They have very definite ideas on any given piece they read. This one *is* funny; this one *isn't*—and how did it ever come to get printed? This can work in the humorist's favor as well as to his disadvantage. When a friend *voluntarily* compliments me on something he's read that I've written, I feel safe in taking for granted that he really means it. No friend, however close, will tell you you're funny when he doesn't honestly think so. I've found *that* out.

So-o-o—how do you go about writing and selling the short prose item? If I had a foolproof blueprint, I'd either keep it to myself or demand full ownership of the State of Texas for it. First of all, you get an idea. It comes to you or it doesn't. Not so long ago, it occurred to me how reluctant people are to come out with the bald truth. They edge up to it in roundabout ways. After a while one gets to detect the method. So here is a shortie of mine that appeared in the "Look on the Light Side" page of *Look:*

QUESTIONS THAT FREEZE ME

"If I drove on a flat tire for just a quarter of a mile or so, it wouldn't matter, would it, dear?"

"What do termites look like, dear?"

"Would it hurt your tennis racket if it got left out in the rain, Dad?"

Observed Sir Francis Bacon, "A man with wife and children hath given hostages to fortune." True, no doubt, but a man with wife and children has an advantage if he wants to write humor. He has a universal subject—so many other men have wives and children. The following is mostly about children, and appeared on the "Post Scripts" page of *The Saturday Evening Post* when our daughter was in the second grade. I believe something akin to this phenomenon has been observed by most parents of second-grade girls:

YOU MEAN YOU MADE THAT ALL BY YOURSELF?

There is one undeniable advantage in having a daughter in the second grade of grammar school—the arts-and-crafts course teaches her to make a number of articles which are absolutely indispensable around the house.

Every week she comes home with some new treasure she has made with her own hands. Among them these items:

Shoelace rack. This is a block of wood containing two hooks. You hang it on the wall. Each night you take the laces out of your shoes and hang them up on the rack. It makes them last much longer.

Toothbrush cover. No longer do my wife and I resort to the unsanitary practice of leaving nude toothbrushes exposed to dust and germs. After each ablution we cover the bristles with the handy little cotton cover sewn by Patsy's own hand. She says that when she gets in the third grade they will let her make them with slide fasteners.

Paper weights. If any papers blow off my desk, I have only myself to blame, what with the availability of nine different paper weights which have accumulated during the past year. My favorite is a large rock, painted blue, on which a cut-out of Mickey Mouse is superimposed. However, I also foresee use for that old stove lid, if the varnish ever dries.

Golf-ball case. Golf balls are obviously going to last longer if kept in a case with separate compartments so that they cannot knock against one another. Thanks to my daughter, I have a beautiful twelve-ball number in heavy cardboard with my initials tastefully painted over a legend which formerly read "Best-Laid. Grade A."

Napkin rings. These are easily made by removing the top and bottom from the small cans that contain concentrated frozen fruit juices. I am happy to announce that our family has a complete set of rings including orange, grapefruit, orange and grapefruit, and pineapple.

But children keep growing. Half a dozen years later, our daughter was in junior high school, and we observed another phenomenon—again, I trust, a universal one: Parents are always having to sign permission slips for various extra-curricular activities. From this came another piece in "Look on the Light Side." And just for the fun of it, I decided to make my wife co-author. Naturally, she received half the profits. That goes without saying.

I've Probably Forgotten Something

Before the school year is over, our daughter will have brought home dozens of documents requesting our signed permission for her to take part in various activities. Wonder if we could clear all this up at once?

To the principal, teachers, nurses, coaches, etc. of Elmwood School:

We, the undersigned, hereby grant permission for our daughter, Patsy, to:

Have her teeth examined.

Take lessons on any string, reed, or brass musical instrument she can lift.

Have a daily extra helping of chocolate milk in the cafeteria.

Join the advanced class in gymnastics and tumbling.

Visit any art or natural history museum, factory, library, major-league ball park, freight yard, bird sanctuary, legislative assembly, zoo, historical shrine or monument within a radius of 75 miles, and to take along for lunch and spending money a sum not to exceed $2.

Join any social, scientific, cultural or athletic group not listed as subversive by the Attorney General of the United States.

Mary Virginia Cummings
Parke Cummings

The previous pieces are examples of subjects that are pretty much timeless. But sometimes we get ideas from a new phenomenon, and one that may be transient. You've seen dozens of pieces about television. Ten years ago one of these might have been about the only family in the neighborhood with a set—and how all the neighbors would drop in, usurp the comfortable chairs and lap up the host's liquor. Such a piece wouldn't have too much point today, since practically everyone has a set (except the very, *very* rich, as far as I can make out).

But in the past couple of years, we've had a spate of Westerns, with emphasis on the "adult" Western and the more complicated characters who are supposed to people it. On this perhaps temporary phase of TV, I worked up virtually a burlesque type of piece for the "Sweet and Sour" page of *Maclean's* of Canada:

How to Tell the Players in an Adult Western

Television, this season, will feature more Westerns than ever—Adult Westerns. An Adult Western is one where character is depicted more subtly. The Bad Guys aren't *entirely* bad or the Good Guys entirely good—as is the case in the Non-Adult Western. You can look for the following gradations this season:

Much more bad than good:

Rustles cattle, corrupts sheriff, ogles women, cusses terribly. But refuses to cheat at poker.

Somewhat worse than better:

Pulls crooked deals, rides horses too hard, gets drunk. But very kind to children and a wonderful cook.

Slightly on good side:

Befriends helpless women, never swears, shaves regularly. But uses marked cards, and gives sheriff the hotfoot.

Great guy but has bad flaw:

Sober, industrious, honest, risks life to thwart bank hold-up, train hold-up, saloon hold-up. But plays slot machines, and is always broke.

Tough to figure out:

Won't steal cattle but steals horses. Chews tobacco but wacky over beautiful sunsets. Gentleman with blondes, but wolf with brunettes. Adores cats, but kicks dogs. Pays all debts, but makes counterfeit money.

I'm looking forward to an Adult Western with all the characters in the last category. I'll bet it will give me more to think about than *Hamlet*.

Getting back to a subject which will probably outlast adult Westerns, we have the week-end guest—specifically, the kind who leaves something behind when he departs and asks you to mail it to him. I figured out how I would like to handle such a character, and did so as follows— only in my imagination, of course. This, first printed in *This Week*, ran a bit longer, and was then reprinted in *The Reader's Digest*. It was also reprinted in a number of their foreign editions, so I may have been right in thinking that a forgetful week-end guest is one in any language.

Strong Medicine for Careless Guests

When friends visit us in our house in the country they're apt to leave various articles behind when they depart, after which they write and ask me to mail them back to them. None of them ever repeats this offense, however. I am allergic to wrapping up stuff and lugging it to the post office, and I have devised a system to break them of this careless and irritating habit.

What I do is cheerfully cooperate. Let me illustrate with how I handled Ed Hamilton, who left a pair of shoes after a week-end last October. The minute I received his request to mail them I answered.

October 18

Dear Ed: Got your letter. I was wondering how you could have left your shoes behind. Did you go home barefoot? I hadn't noticed.   Parke

Ed replied that he hadn't gone home barefoot. He had taken an extra pair of shoes, and he wanted me to mail them to him. Again I cooperated.

November 7

Dear Ed: I'm all set to send those shoes back to you, but first I've got to know which pair you left here, the ones you were wearing when you arrived or the extra pair you brought along? Parke

Ed wrote back, demanding, for Pete's sake, what difference did it make whether he left the pair he was wearing or the spare pair? He wanted those shoes. My own reply was considerably more courteous.

November 23

Dear Ed: The reason I asked was because I wanted to know what color the shoes were. Please let me know, because I want to return them to you *at once*. Hope your family is feeling fit. Parke

The next letter from Ed struck me as a bit abrupt. It just said "Brown."

After I recovered from a cold that had laid me up I promptly wrote him another letter.

December 17

Dear Ed: Now we're getting somewhere! I figured they were either brown or black, and it's good to know definitely. The shoes are as good as yours. Just tell me where you left them and I'll send them without delay. Best wishes to you and the family for Christmas. Parke

Soon afterward I received another letter: "In the guest room, stupid! Where else?" Not a word of Christmas greeting from him. However, I ignored this rudeness when I next wrote.

January 11

Dear Ed: Great news! I found your shoes. Size 10½, eh? Don't bother to confirm this, as I want to get them off to you without a moment's unnecessary delay. Unfortunately I mislaid your earlier letters and I forgot whether you want me to send them by railway express or parcel post. Parke

In his reply Ed said he didn't give a damn how I sent them just as long as I got those shoes off in a hurry.

As soon as I could, I wrote him back.

February 18

Dear Ed: It sure looks as though you'd be receiving those shoes any day now. I've decided on parcel post. Do you want me to mark the package "Fragile"? Please give me this information so I can get them off promptly. Warmest regards to you and all your lovely family.   Parke

Shortly afterward I got a wire from Ed saying, "Quit stalling and send those shoes."

A few days ago I actually mailed them. My guess is that Ed will be less apt to leave his property behind when he makes future visits, and the same holds true of other guests with whom I have cooperated. And it's highly gratifying to know that I've never once addressed a single unkind word to any of them.

How many points these examples illustrate, I can't say, but I think they do point up that humor is a wide field, its subjects can be found just about anywhere, and you can't single out any one type of person to write it. The hypothetical lawyer or housewife I've mentioned could just as well have written all of these pieces as I.

MARY T. STEYN, *Associate Editor of* The Reader's Digest, *joined the staff of this magazine in 1938 and has been at work there ever since. In charge of the* Digest's *Editorial Correspondence Department, Mrs. Steyn is in close touch with the magazine's readers and is constantly on the watch for usable article ideas, material worthy of reprinting, etc.*

THE READER'S DIGEST AS A FILLER MARKET

By MARY T. STEYN

A woman I met at a gathering recently was so quietly serene and so lovely to look at that I was surprised to learn she is the mother of seven children, the youngest three years old. When two of her girls joined us, both about 12, I remarked that it must have been hard having them so close together.

"Not at all," she said. "We adopted Joanie two years ago."

"Good heavens," I burst out, "didn't you have enough of your own?"

"Yes, of course," she said simply. "But Joanie had no one at all."

> Estelle Zuzack
> (St. Louis, Mo.)

A friend living in an isolated Montana mining town suspected that she wasn't getting the best dental care. Her first trip to a competent dentist in Butte confirmed her suspicions. After a thorough examination the dentist asked but one question:

"Been doing your own work?"

Mrs. Conrad LaSalle
(Hamilton, Mont.)

A husband-and-wife photography team we know shoot their pictures together, do their developing and printing together—in fact, they're together 24 hours of the day. We wondered how they managed to keep up such good working relations.

"Well, frankly," the wife said, "it wouldn't work out if one of us didn't have a good disposition."

"Which one?" we asked.

"Oh," she laughed, "we take turns!"

Elizabeth Jeter
(Dallas, Texas)

While having lunch at a restaurant in Nevada, I was idly watching a woman play the slot machines. As she ran out of coins, she would come over to the counter and ask the proprietor for change. On her third trip she commented acidly, "Don't these machines ever pay?"

"Oh, yes, ma'am," he said. "They pay the lights. They pay the rent. They pay the help. They pay real good, ma'am!"

Ada Graham
(Thermopolis, Wyo.)

When a friend of mine went in to pay a Washington, D. C., obstetrician for bringing his youngster into the world, he noticed that she—for it was a woman doctor—consulted a little black book. "That will be fifty dollars," she said.

After he'd written the check he asked why she had needed the little book to determine the fee.

"I jot down what the father asks when I come out of the delivery room—it's always either one of two questions. If you had said, 'Is it a boy or a girl?' my fee would have

been seventy-five dollars. But you said, 'How is my wife?'
And that makes it an even fifty."

Mrs. A. M. R. Lawrence, Jr.
(Manassas, Va.)

The above, all published within the past year or so in the famous "Life in These United States" department of *The Reader's Digest,* are the sort of everyday-life anecdotes readers have come to connect with the *Digest.* They narrate incidents that might have happened almost anywhere and yet there's something a little special about each one of them. A "Life in These United States" story may afford the reader a swift insight into human nature, throw light on some common characteristic of men or of women, prompt a kindly chuckle at an individual foible or a sympathetic grin at the plight of a human being in a familiar dilemma. "Life" stories may even teach a lesson, if the moral is pointed gently, as in Mrs. Jeter's story quoted above.

These stories, which ordinarily don't exceed 300 words, almost invariably say a lot in a little. Articles have been written about the American disease of automobilitis, but the point was made more succinctly by Mrs. Winifred Enright of Buffalo in a recent issue of the *Digest:*

> I never realized how seldom I went out without the car until I overheard an observation made by my daughter. She and a friend were approaching the back door when the other girl said, "Maybe nobody's home."
> "Oh, yes, there is," my daughter replied. "The car's in —and we never leave the car home alone."

"Life in These United States," one of the popular continuing features of *The Reader's Digest,* is made up entirely of material contributed by the magazine's readers and has appeared almost every month since inauguration of the department in March 1943. Doubtless, many readers of this book have at one time or another sent in a story in the hope of earning the $100 payment offered for acceptable 300-word anecdotes.

In the 15 years of the department's existence, the number of contributions has climbed to astronomical figures: currently, "Life in These United States" receives more than 20,000 pieces of mail monthly, many of the envelopes containing multiple submissions. Outside contributors also send in some 10,000 submissions directed to other departments of the magazine, many including collections of clippings, groups of original epigrams, "Picturesque Speech," etc. Altogether the total of individual items submitted runs up to as much as half a million yearly.

These formidable statistics seem enough to discourage any would-be contributor to the pages of the world's most widely read magazine. But there is no real reason for discouragement. The solicitation of material for various departments of the *Digest* is in no sense a contest in which one's chances may diminish as the number of contestants increases. It is simply a part of the continuing search for the best possible editorial material.

Experience has taught the editors that in their own readers is a never-failing vein of editorial gold, truly the mother lode as far as excerpt material goes. As a result, *The Reader's Digest* is perhaps the most "contributed to" of any large general magazine. Few readers are aware, as they leaf through the *Digest's* pages in search of the bright quips, amusing or heart-warming anecdotes and thought-provoking quotes that enliven each issue, that well over half of the 120 or so short items in any month's *Digest* have been sent in to us from "outside." A detailed study of the excerpt material gathered together for three recent issues of the magazine reveals that of 395 short items used, 247 were sent in by outside contributors. This is approximately 65% of the total, a statistic that should provide real encouragement for free-lance contributors.

It is obvious that a considerable amount of work lies between receipt of the annual half-million contributed items and publication of approximately 1500 of them each year. The generous payments to contributors of acceptable stories for "Life in These United States" and other features represent only a part of the editorial expense involved: four staff members inside the office spend full time on fillers. Two others spend part of their time on departments. These editors are supplemented by about a dozen part-time workers outside.

The handling of "Life in These United States" contributions typifies the procedure. Outside readers do the first sifting of contributed material, holding out every item for which there seems the remotest chance for acceptance. Each one then sends the remainder of her mail on to a partner who goes over it again, drawing out still more submissions that strike her as possibilities. These, too, are mailed in to Pleasantville.

From the collection of 1000 to 1500 selected items on hand at the end of any given month, the editor in charge of "Life" selects a group that promises to make up a lively and appealing department. Some alternates are added to provide for the inevitable loss of a few stories that don't, for one reason or another, meet with final editorial approval. The group is then handed over to the editor-in-charge of the issue for that month, who may wield his own axe before submitting the culled and edited group for final o.k.

In looking for usable items, what is it that each member

of the staff is searching for in the stories our readers send in and in his own reading of newspapers, magazines and books? Requirements for the various departments differ, of course. They are briefly indicated in the announcements that appear in the magazine each month, on the page entitled "Have You an Amusing Anecdote?" But the characteristics of a usable story are exceedingly difficult to define and the best way to determine them is to study the material appearing in the magazine itself. (The newly published *Treasury of Wit and Humor,* an anthology of the *Digest's* best short humorous material with samplings from the various departments, should be useful to anyone studying the magazine's requirements.) A strenuous effort is made to avoid stereotypes; an occasional quip may even be selected simply because it *doesn't* sound like *The Reader's Digest.* But still, the *Digest* itself is the best teacher, and the contributor should go over several copies before sending in material. He should note especially the various department headings and group titles. There is a three-page office list of working headings for excerpts, including such frequently used titles as "Classified Classics," "Deft Definitions," "Eye-Openers," "Footnotes to History," "Hollywood Round-Up," "Innocents Abroad," "Letters Perfect," "Office Daze," "Points to Ponder," and "Surprise Endings." Be on the watch for new items or anecdotes that might be used under these already developed titles.

Occasional departments bear watching too. Contributions to "Man's Best Friend," and "Wild Wisdom," for example, will always receive consideration. These features appear only once or twice a year, largely because outstanding material for them is not available in sufficient quantity to run them more often than that.

You will probably direct your contribution to a specific department, and indeed you are asked to do so. But don't worry about your story being overlooked entirely if it doesn't fit the needs of the department to which it was addressed. Outstanding stories are passed from editor to editor, and all concerned make an effort to find the proper niche for an anecdote or quote that has genuine appeal.

Payment is made on the basis of the item's final disposition. Thus a story submitted to "Life in These United States" but used as one of three items under a group heading such as "Well Known Human Race" would not win its contributor $100 (the regular payment for accepted "Life in These United States" stories) unless the anecdote in its published form was 20 lines long. The payment for original material used in "Personal Glimpses," "Laughter, the Best Medicine," and elsewhere is $5 per *Digest* two-column line.

Quite a large proportion of *Digest* excerpts are reprinted from other published sources. These items are found in a variety of ways. Staff members covering hundreds of small magazines and house organs, small-circulation newspapers, etc., locate many of the items that are used. Also, certain outside contributors have been immensely helpful in this area, some of them working hard at the job of contributing reprint items to the *Digest*.

Likely sources for outside contributors are local newspapers, non-syndicated columns, regional publications. Excellent items have been found in the encyclopedia, in annual reports, in the folders that sometimes accompany telephone and milk bills, in advertisements and pamphlets. Radio, television, the movies, and the theater often yield usable material. Some of the very best fillers have been stories told at a party or fragments of overheard conversation.

Less likely as excerpt source material are the national magazines. These are exhaustively covered by the *Digest* staff and their excerpts, departments, cartoons, etc., as well as the full-length articles are subjected to careful scrutiny. Joke books are poor sources to draw on—our staff has almost certainly beaten the non-staffer to any such obvious possibility. Other books, though, may yield "Quotable Quotes," epigrams, items for "Picturesque Speech," "Points to Ponder," etc. Even though the *Digest's* book department working in cooperation with the *Condensed Books* staff covers practically all current books, still they are looking primarily for material to be used at length—as *Digest* Book Sections or in the quarterly volumes of *Condensed Books*. They may well overlook the sort of brief item under discussion here. In the same way, members of the magazine staff, covering the nation's vast monthly periodical output, sometimes fail to notice, in the body of an unusable article, a good short quote, a "Personal Glimpse," or an item for "Laughter, the Best Medicine."

In submitting previously published material, remember to give full sources including page references, with place of publication for newspapers, whose names often duplicate each other. It is helpful to have submissions pasted or typed singly on separate sheets, with the name and address of the contributor on each sheet. This facilitates the above-described passing about of items for consideration for different departments of the magazine.

But what *is* it that sells a story to the *Digest?* One member of the staff tells me he has one general rule: He never passes over anything that makes him either laugh out loud or feel a lump in his throat. These are subjective reactions, it's true, and remember that they are reactions of an experienced editor. As such, they are indicative. The doctored up "gag," the contrived story, won't usually prompt this sort of direct emotional response. If you find yourself laughing uproariously and wholeheartedly at a humorous experience, your own or a friend's, stop and ask yourself if you haven't just been exposed to a bit of genuine "Life in These United States." If the answer is yes, get to a typewriter right away and set the story down in rough draft while its details are clear in your mind. If the story concerns someone else, you should ask yourself *how* you were laughing. Were you sympathetic with the narrator?

The *Digest* editorial staff ordinarily fails to find anything very funny in practical jokes or in stories whose humor results from the fact of a person's race or from some physical handicap. A large proportion of rejected stories fall in these general categories.

Frequently received (by the thousands!) but not often used are stories turning on the bright sayings or clever actions of children. There are few parents who can resist the temptation to talk about their children, and such stories often have undeniable appeal. But to be selected for publication they must be *really outstanding*. After all, there'd be little point in printing a story about a child who struck the reader as being no brighter or more charming than his own young hopeful.

Every batch of excerpt contributions contains also a certain proportion of "oldies," stories that are familiar to the staff because of their frequent submission over the years. At one time a group of these was published under the appropriate title "The Lasting Laugh." Indeed it is a tribute to their genuine humor that stories like the one about the child with the potty stuck on his head and the lady who spied her new flowered hat adorning a relative's grave continue to come in year after year, usually told as the personal experience of the contributor. But their familiarity does make these anecdotes unusable and they are discarded.

Also summarily discarded is the frankly pornographic story. Here again we are involved in considerations of good taste. Just as stories turning on racial characteristics, on physical handicaps or on cruelty of one sort or another seem to us to offend good taste, so certain sex stories are unthinkable for *The Reader's Digest*. But the fact that a story has sex overtones does not in itself rule it out. Since sex is a part of human life, stories dealing cleverly and honestly with it are acceptable to the *Digest*, as they are today to most general magazines.

The Reader's Digest needs and wants good filler material. Readers of this book are urged to keep the magazine in mind as a market for their very best short items.

RICHARD ARMOUR, *who leads the double life of a college professor and a popular writer, has published over 5,000 pieces of verse and prose in more than 100 magazines. Now Professor of English at Scripps College and the Claremont Graduate School, he has written scholarly books of biography and literary criticism. But he is best known for his light verse, collected in such volumes as* Light Armour *and* Nights With Armour; *his* Writing Light Verse; *and his best-selling satires on history and literature, including* It All Started With Columbus, It All Started With Europa, It All Started With Eve, Twisted Tales From Shakespeare, *and* It All Started With Marx.

IV

CRACKING THE QUIP

BY RICHARD ARMOUR

The shortest of all the short forms of writing is the quip—also known as the epigram, the aphorism, the saying, the saw, the wisecrack, the filler, and the quote. There may be a little difference between the quip or wisecrack and the epigram or aphorism, because the former is likely to be humorous and the latter wise. But humor and wisdom are, in my opinion, akin. A wise saying can be funny and a funny saying can be wise. Both involve either witty twisting of language or sharp perception of human nature, or both.

It has always seemed to me that there is a relationship between the I.Q. and what might be called the H.Q., or Humor Quotient. People who are slow to catch a joke are likely to be slow to catch anything, except maybe a cold. Certainly the smartest characters in Shakespeare's plays are some of his clowns and fools, and if the kings had listened to their advice they would have been alive at the end of the fifth act.

So there is a certain amount of wisdom, or at least human understanding, in a good quip. Moreover, it is a type of writing, the ultimate in condensation, which has a long and honorable history, going back to Confucius, the morals at the end of Aesop's Fables, and the memorable sentences, good enough to stand alone, in the essays of Montaigne and Bacon. The French, for example the Duc de la Rochefoucauld, have excelled at the brief, witty, quotable epigram, but the Americans have done all right with Benjamin Franklin and Mark Twain and Ambrose Bierce and Will Rogers.

I have said that the quip (and I shall henceforth use the shortest of the several terms mentioned above) is the shortest of all the short forms of writing. How short is short? Well, a quip is rarely longer than one sentence, and it may be no more than a verbless phrase. Calculated by the word, it is probably the most lucrative kind of writing today, for a quip will usually bring ten dollars from any of the better magazines. A ten-word quip would thus pay the writer a dollar a word. A five-word quip would bring the rate up to two dollars a word. Reprints may multiply this figure many times over, though there is a tendency for quips not only to be used again without payment, but to be used without the author's name, or with someone else's name. "It's a wise crack that knows its own father," as someone (you see, I don't know who) once quipped about the quip.

Since the quip brings so much for so little, it would seem that one could quickly get rich by sitting down and writing maybe a hundred quips a day. But, though quips to some extent can be manufactured, they cannot be turned out at any such rate, or not for long. It is an odd thing, but for five or six years I rode high on a wave of quips. All I had to do was to push my brain around for half an hour and I would produce six or eight. Before the vein, or the artery, wore out, I had written more than two thousand, a good proportion of which I sold and many of which were reprinted in *The Reader's Digest*. But suddenly I got so I could push my brain for an hour, push it until it was out of shape, and produce maybe one quip or half a quip (a half-witticism) or none at all. Nowadays a quip comes occasionally, if I work hard enough at it, but I seem to have lost the ability to produce on a large scale. Perhaps there is a fruitful period, a time when quips are hanging there, ripe for the picking. Then the snows set in. If winter comes, can spring be far behind? It can.

But perhaps your mind is just at the state when, if you stir it around a little, the quips will start dropping as they once did for me and as they may again. There is a large demand for quips, which are used up fast by magazines like *The Saturday Evening Post, The American Legion Magazine, Look,* and *Coronet,* and by such daily newspaper features as "Pepper and Salt" in *The Wall Street Journal.* Although *The Reader's Digest* usually reprints quips from the various magazines, the editors will accept really good ones that are sent in direct.

How to get started at quip writing? One thing you

might do is to look at those that have been published, carefully study the successful product. Some 30,000 quotations, many of which are the type that might be called quips, may be found in H. L. Mencken's *New Dictionary of Quotations*. A handier collection is Frederick B. Wilcox's *A Little Book of Aphorisms*. An ingenious, dictionary-arranged mass of quips with higher humor content and less literary value is Evan Esar's amusing *Esar's Comic Dictionary*. Of recent years Esar's quips have been syndicated, appearing one a day, as if to give the reader his essential humor vitamin, in many newspapers. In addition to these collections, it would be a good idea to examine the current magazines, both to look at models and to study markets.

A special reason for reading others' quips is that these will frequently furnish the starting point for one's own. Many modern quips are merely new treatments of familiar sayings, common expressions, clichés. What one does is to start with the known and try to emerge with something unexpected but still plausible and pat. See what has been done, for example, with the age-old observation, an antique but not antiquated quip, "People who live in glass houses shouldn't throw stones." Under *glass houses,* Esar lists four variations on the theme, including "People who live in glass houses shouldn't throw parties" and "People who live in glass houses shouldn't." The first of these, which continues the familiar saying, but in an unexpected direction, might be described as a "twisted cliché." The second, which ends abruptly before the saying is concluded, and yet makes sense and brings out a new meaning, might be called a "truncated cliché." To these should be added the "extended cliché," in which the common expression is untwisted and uncut, but is carried on to an entirely new conclusion, as in "Cleanliness is next to godliness, but in children it's next to impossible."

On this "People who live in glass houses" expression, I might add that Phyllis McGinley has neatly turned it around in the title of her book of light verse, *Stones from a Glass House.* And I can think of still another twist: "People who live in stone houses shouldn't throw glasses."

An amusing example of what can be done with the truncated cliché is a quip (the source of which I cannot now place) in which, by cutting off but a single letter, the author brought out a fresh (very fresh) and possibly appropriate meaning. The one I have in mind is: "Having wonderful time, wish you were *her.*" An example of a twisted cliché in which only one word is altered is: "Many hands *want* light work." Or, with some truth, it could be: "Many hands make work." So also: "A watched pot never boils over."

This last one is perhaps more nearly an extended cliché, although it is extended by only one word. This is my own favorite kind of quip, the kind of thing I do most habitually. Thus a bit of thought on "a man's man" gave me "A man's man is very often a woman's too," which went to *Ladies' Home Journal.* The expression "to carry a tune," having gone through the perverting process of my mind, led me to the observation that "Some people can carry a tune, but they seem to stagger under the load," which was used as a filler in *The Saturday Evening Post.* Ditto the word play in "When it comes to eating, you can sometimes help yourself more by helping yourself less" and "People who are really bright do a lot of reflecting."

Word play, as in the above, can also be the basis of a piece of light verse, or the clincher at the end. So it is not surprising that what I first jotted down as a quip may eventually come out instead as the last line of a quatrain. As Shakespeare almost said, "The word play's the thing."

Quips often take the form of definitions, though hardly the sort found in a dictionary. The prevailing tone is usually cynical; the wit or humor derives from incongruity between the lofty or at least respectable word and the crass, realistic "definition" of it. Ambrose Bierce was one of the earlier masters of this technique, and he was followed by H. L. Mencken. Consider Bierce's definition of "to be positive," which he says is "to be mistaken at the top of one's voice." Or Mencken on "hope": "A pathological belief in the occurrence of the impossible"; and "immorality": "The morality of those who are having a better time." Most of the good ones are anonymous; for instance, "Diplomat: A man who remembers a lady's birthday but forgets her age" and "Expert: An ordinary man away from home giving advice." One of mine, with a little word play thrown in, is "Agreeable people are people who agree with you"; another is "Adolescence is when children start trying to bring up their parents." Cynicism is generally but not always the rule. The definition-type quip can also be written pretty straight, and with an element of the figurative or poetic, as in "A gossip is a woman who warms herself by the fire of other people's burning ears," or "Wisdom is knowledge that has been cured in the brine of tears."

So many humorous definitions begin "A woman is . . ." that a quip might almost be defined as "A short saying which begins 'A woman is. . . .'" But other favorites are "Middle age is. . . ." and "The good old days were when. . . ." Again, you might say: "The good old days were when nobody referred to the good old days."

Definition-quips have sometimes been strung together to make an entire book, as in Ambrose Bierce's *The Devil's Dictionary*. More recently John Bailey, after contributing many of these to *The Saturday Evening Post*, made a delightful book of them. Frequently you will find a dozen or so, by different authors or by one author, brought together in a little cluster in *The Reader's Digest, Redbook*, or some other magazine. Not long ago I compiled a short feature for *Today's Living*, the Sunday magazine of the *New York Herald Tribune*. Made up of quips of mine that had not been previously published, it was called "Definitions Not in the Dictionary":

Balanced diet: what you eat at buffet suppers.
Bookkeeper: person who fails to return the book you lent him.
Buckshot: what a dollar is, these days, after you have bought something.
Capital punishment: spending the summer in Washington, D. C.
Climate: weather that has got into a rut.
Dogma: a mother dog.
Friendly argument: one that has just started.
Gossip: a person to whom no news is bad news.
Picture hat: hat worn by a woman in front of you at the movies, that keeps you from seeing the picture.
Sweater girl: girl who makes the men tend to her knitting.
Trade secrets: what women do.
Turkey gobbler: person who eats a lot of turkey.
Vacation bound: what you are for the rest of the year after you have paid for your vacation.
Waiter: person who jealously guards the restaurant's water supply.
Wife: lie detector without wires.

Frequently a quip involves an original sort of comparison or differentiation. What is called for, in the first instance, is a fresh and colorful simile in which there is an essential, if somewhat exaggerated, likeness between the subject and the thing with which it is compared. Thus Don Marquis: "Publishing a volume of verse is like dropping a rose petal down the Grand Canyon and waiting for the echo." Or the anonymous "A good speech, like a woman's skirt, should be long enough to cover the subject and short enough to create interest." A still more fertile field is the sort of quip that starts out, "The difference between. . . ." Examples are: "The difference between shortsightedness and nearsightedness is that nearsightedness is correctible"; and, with possibly a little more surprise: "The difference between playing golf for the game and for the exercise is about ten strokes." However grotesque the comparison, the completed statement should make sense, and plenty of it.

While a quip may contain word play, or even such a coinage as "break-a-brac" or "Santa Claustrophobia," it will get along very nicely if it is simply a wise observation on life, stated succinctly. Balanced phraseology may help, as in Oscar Wilde's "It is better to be beautiful than to be good, but it is better to be good than to be ugly," or in C. C. Colton's "If you would be known and not know, vegetate in a village; if you would know, and not be known, live in a city." But a straightforward statement, full of shirtsleeve rather than stuffed-shirt philosophy, can be quite effective. For my own part, I have managed to ring the editorial bell with such simple truisms as: "It is easy for people who are not hungry to have good table manners"; "When people say they are giving you their opinion for what it is worth, you can be sure they are putting a high value on it" (in which will be recognized a trace of the extended cliché); and "There is some consolation in the fact that, even though your dreams don't come true, neither do your nightmares." One that combines home-spun wisdom with word play and surprise ending is: "Every young man has two good openings—his ears." But the important thing in all these is the common sense content.

The idea need not be new—in fact I sometimes wonder whether a wholly new idea is possible any more. Rather, it should be a universally accepted thought which is stated with new force and compression. As Dr. Johnson, a lexicographer and an expert quipster himself, once stated about aphorisms, a quip consists "not so much in the expression of some rare or abstruse statement as in the comprehension of some obvious and useful truth in a few words." It follows that the subjects of quips must be those of general and everyday interest: love, money, youth and age, politics, health, religion, friendship, success, and so on.

To illustrate the variety of quips, I set down a few of the good, bad, and indifferent ones from my files:

Some speakers cover a subject so thoroughly that you can't see a trace of it.

A sweeping statement can raise a lot of dust.

You can have your close friends; give me generous ones.

When a man hasn't a leg to stand on, he is likely to make some lame excuses.

Some of us might care for pets more if we didn't have to care for them so much.

In a traffic accident, the one who is right is not always the one who is left.

The man who divorces a talkative wife and remarries may just be getting his second wind.

To the pessimist, some people are born lucky; to the optimist, everyone is lucky to have been born.

Tact is the art of saying what you think only when it is what others wish to hear.

Some people have a hard row to hoe, and no hoe.

To the insomniac, it's a great life if you don't waken.

The shoe shine boy is one fellow who makes money hand over foot.

When youth burns the midnight oil, these days, it is usually in the crankcase.

Some people make spectacles of themselves with a couple of glasses.

Of the above quips, some were sold and some were not. If you can tell which are which, you may have the makings of a quip writer—or an editor.

Short as it is—perhaps because it is so short—a quip takes even more polishing than most kinds of writing. Extraneous words must be deleted. Weak words must be replaced by more precise or more colorful words. Unless the quip is too timely to keep, you might well let it settle and ripen and age. Although it cannot improve of itself with time, the writer may, with time, see that it needs improving, and discover how to improve it.

As for submitting quips, they can be typed individually on sheets of paper or on three-by-five cards. Or they can be submitted several on a page, with enough space between them so that the editor may, if he accepts one, clip it off and return the rest. But this is unimportant. A good quip will shine through any wrapper. The main thing is to write lots and lots of them. With quips, as with years, the first hundred are the hardest.

GURNEY WILLIAMS has sold humorous essays to virtually every major magazine during the past 30 years, and has been on the buying end since 1932. At Look Magazine, *he edits the "Light Side" page, to which he frequently contributes under the name of Fred Houston. But all his own material, he says, must be approved by* Look's *Editorial Board and much of it is turned down. "My sympathy is very much for the writer," he adds, "because I have experienced—and still do experience—his rejection-depression and acceptance-elation."*

V

AN EDITOR'S VIEWPOINT

By Gurney Williams

If someone offered me two dollars to dream up the equivalent of the businessman's THINK sign for humorists, I'd suggest RESTRAINT, for the reason that the outstanding weakness of the material I reject is over-emphasis. Writers I have known take the "Boy, am I funny!" approach, trying to overcome an editor's steadfast resistance to the bombastic and wearisome clown of letters.

Let's begin with a simple thing like the exclamation point. Many professionals and most amateurs seem to feel that the liberal use of ! ! ! ! !s will punch up flagging material. For me, exclamation points shout too much, like the baggy-pants, loud-mouthed comedians of burlesque.

The better humor markets are not media in which screaming comics are regarded with favor.

Here's an epigram as it might be written by a "bang-point" enthusiast: "Life can be very unpleasant when you get into the 80's, especially if a motorcycle cop is following you!" If that last punctuation mark makes it funnier, wouldn't two of them make it even more amusing? Obviously not. Restraint, the low-key treatment, is far more effective.

This is not to imply that the exclamation point is obsolete. It can, for one thing, create a sense of enthusiasm necessary for a certain type of characterization, as in the following item from a series of sketches titled, "There's No Use Getting All Steamed Up."

> "Listen, Harry; I just put in a complete stereophonic outfit and it's out of this world! Two 50-watt Woofle-Craft amplifiers, matching 12-inch coaxial Wow-Audio speakers and a Tweet-Sound pickup arm on a Flutterberg turntable! You ought to hear *Rachmaninoff's Second Concerto* on this rig! Fantastic!"
> To which Harry says simply:
> "My hobby is stamps."

The exclamation points enable us to feel the hi-fi enthusiast's fanaticism; we can almost hear his excited recital. In contrast is the stamp collector's flat statement.

Immoderate use of italics, too, can trip an unwary humor writer. In the following epigram the italics are superfluous but could easily have been used by a humorist who makes too much of a point of making a point. "An old-timer is a man who once was a celebrity *because he won $100 on a quiz program.*" The same goes for capital letters. You might call it unnecessary impact.

This tendency to accentuate the obvious—the "ha, ha,

get it?" business—does not improve a flimsy idea and only weakens a good one. Perhaps it might be well to keep in mind that your reader is not an oaf who must have everything explained to him. Consider him to be your peer in intelligence; let the slow-witted character spell things out if he must.

What do you write, or want to write—epigrams, light verse, short prose humor, all three?

If you have a flair for both epigrams and verse, one can be played against the other. That is, a pungent comment, or epigram, can often be stretched into a poem (and a bigger check). One of my tests for a piece of verse is to ignore the rhyme formation and see if the bare idea stands on its own feet. The result is what I call Williams' Law: "If a four-line poem can be rewritten as an amusing epigram, it's a sound quatrain, and vice versa." Let's see how this checks out.

EPIGRAM: We know a lot of suburbanites who have discovered that trees grow on money.

VERSE: The country dweller's one who knows
    (To him, this isn't funny)
The dough he spends on saplings shows
    That trees do grow on money.

CONVERSELY: There's one sure thing:
Your phone won't ring
And disturb a deserved slumber,
If you have a son
Under twenty-one,
Who calls up a real cool number.

EPIGRAM: If you want to keep the phone from ringing while you take a two-hour nap, just ask your teen-age daughter to call up one of her friends.

However, if the transition from one form to the other seems contrived, don't labor over it; stay with the original construction. The free-and-easy bit is generally more successful.

As a verse buyer, I find that writers too often depend upon a clever rhyme scheme to bolster a limp idea, or no idea. Rhyming the last words in every line is a favorite experiment which goes like this:

> I tore my pants
> On thorny plants
> And my wife rants
> At my expanse.
> I'm glad the ants—

—and so on, usually to nowhere.

There's a place for contrived *words* in rhyme, though, not only because the improvisations themselves can be funny but because they give the writer a lot of latitude. "Hi-Fi Ho Hum" was the title of this three-liner:

> I wish so
> That calypso
> Would collapso.

A professor of English might go mad trying to scan this doggerel but it appealed, nevertheless, and was quoted on TV and radio following its appearance in *Look*.

A two-line bit that read:

> Relatives with cameras
> Seldom make you glameras

wound up as a one-line item in *The Reader's Digest* "Picturesque Speech" department minus the title—"The Old Focus at Home"—itself a somewhat pasty gem.

As a rule, a legitimate word like cameras should precede "glameras," which is really no word at all and might distract the customers. They must be conditioned, made receptive, to the unorthodox. If a reader stumbles over a two-liner reading:

> A lot of girls aren't glameras
> Before the TV cameras

he's apt to get irritated and you'll never get famous.

The indestructible pun will, as you probably know, always find a market. Use puns wisely; don't let them use you. Some of your friends and mine verbally overdo this form of humor to the point of intolerable boredom. They'll interrupt a conversation just for the sake of making a pun, whether it's pertinent or not. Usually, it isn't. This failing can beset a writer, too. Again, the RESTRAINT sign.

Comments on the news have a place in the "filler" category, and puns can give them an added lightness. Consider these (the comments are set off here in parentheses):

> In Mobile, Ala., a hen flew into the tax collector's office and laid an egg. (The ordinary taxpayer does this only when he is called in to try to explain a deduction.)

> Two airmen demolished their light plane near Lupin Lodge, Calif., after skimming the tree-tops of a nudist camp. (Contrary to accepted flying procedure, it's obvious they should have been less attentive to the take-off and avoided the strip altogether.)

> The National Macaroni Institute estimates that every American ate an average of 25,000 inches of spaghetti last year. (This obviously does not include yardage lost by incomplete passes.)

From experience, I've learned not to mull over any news item that isn't inherently humorous or does not lend itself easily to a quick quip. Here's a straight one, with no pun needed:

The Soviet Union claims to have produced a camera capable of taking 32,000,000 pictures a second. (Having just viewed our neighbor's vacation slides, we feel pretty certain this invention has been around for some time.)

The subject of news items brings us to the question of timely and topical humor. (Here I use the first definition of the word topical: "pertaining to place.") Timely humor can't be handled well in the big-circulation magazines because of the time lag between the creation of the wheeze and its appearance, five to eight weeks later, on the newsstands. The eternal problem of both writer and editor is to try to determine which of today's events will survive the hiatus.

As to topical affairs, editors of national magazines know there are a lot of readers in Fargo, Fairbanks, Fort Dodge and Filadelfia who don't give a fig about what's hot in, say, Manhattan. A writer, likewise, must avoid provincial thinking, no matter where he lives. This means simply that humorous material must relate to experiences common to the greatest possible number of readers. *The New Yorker* is tops in its field; yet many of its best cartoons and comments, based purely on metropolitan New York situations, are often incomprehensible to the most astute of its out-of-town readers.

This basic premise applies, of course, to all forms of humor. When an idea calls for straight exposition, or narration, make sure the subject matter is of wide interest. If your essay concerning the eccentricities of your grandfather is rejected by every editor in the business, try to look objectively at what seemed to be a "natural." The fact that your grandfather may have had an uncommonly peculiar habit is, to be sure, hilarious to you and your family, but you may find it impossible to amuse your readers with an account of it. They could more easily feel sympathetic towards your grandfather if you told them about his contempt for modern inventions, or the irritations he experienced with any of the facets of living that irritate almost everybody. The three F's—human frailties, foibles and frustrations—make up the meat of the matter. Concentrate on them and you'll *communicate*.

Note the simplicity of this episode, which was published under the title, "How to Open Your Big Yap in Public":

> All of us occasionally find ourselves in tight little embarrassments which call for an appropriate remark. But under stress, we generally find ourselves at a loss for words. You needn't be tongue-tied. Just memorize the simple sentences you'll find in my book called *Crushers*. They've been tailored to fit all the usual situations. Page 86 contains this example:
>
> While driving in traffic, you signal for a right turn but make a left turn by mistake, and a large truck crashes into your fender. The driver—a huge man with cauliflower ears—descends from his cab and lumbers toward you. A crowd gathers.
>
> "Well?" growls the truck driver belligerently. Taking the initiative, you stare steadily at him, and in a loud and even voice you say: "Since when did they start issuing driving permits to mentally retarded orangutans?" There will be a roar of laughter from the bystanders at your sally. This will be followed immediately by a round of applause as the truck driver breaks your nose.
>
> The price of the book is $2.95 and all sales are final.

Following publication of this piece, one reader confessed with some chagrin that he had asked a book dealer for a copy of *Crushers* and had been told it didn't exist. From this I gather (1) that he liked the item enough to want more, or that (2) he had no sense of humor and was taken in by the restrained treatment.

Here, in part, is another way of handling similar everyday annoyances. This was called "Letters I Have Drastically Revised":

Dear County Utilities:
    I have your card notifying me that the gas and electric rates have been raised 60 cents per month. This is an unmitigated outrage. Kindly shut off the service at my residence and have the meters remov—

Dear Director of Internal Revenue:
    Your letter requesting me to appear at your office bearing proof of contributions claimed in my 1956 return strikes me as being a pretty imperious demand from a government employee. As a taxpayer, I feel my civil liberties are endangered, and I flatly refu—

This type of subject matter offers unlimited possibilities and can be presented in many forms.

Short pieces written entirely in dialogue make for easy reading, but dialogue is a tricky commodity. Tyros, especially, have trouble with quotes, and a great deal of supposedly funny conversation reads too awkwardly to be credible. Here's a little horror: "What's that, officer? You say I was doing 75 and you're going to give me a ticket? Well, look at that sign there. It says '75.' Oh—that's the route number?" I'm not exaggerating much; I see even more stilted writing every day.

Assuming you do not find dialogue cumbersome, short conversational sentences, headed by a covering title, are fairly easy to write; but this device has been worked over a great deal and can become static unless one's ingenuity and imagination are fully utilized. You've seen a countless number of such pieces titled, "Things I Wish I Had Said Instead," "Questions I Shouldn't Have Asked" and the like. For example, here in toto is "Honesty is a Tough Policy":

"It has been a lovely evening, but I'm afraid we've stayed much too long."
"You sure have."

*   *   *

"Well, it turned out to be acute appendicitis and the doctor said—but I don't want to bore you."
"Then why do you?"

*   *   *

"So after I finished telling Johnny about the birds and the bees, do you know what he said?"
"No, and I hope I never find out."

*   *   *

"I know I'm not pretty. There are lots prettier girls than me."
"I agree with you."

*   *   *

"That was *Moonlight on the Ganges.* Not bad for only two lessons, was it?"
"It was the most atrocious guitar playing I've ever heard."

*   *   *

"Tell me honestly: Do you think I have a sense of humor?"
"No."

Since there is no real beginning or ending to such pieces, it is wise for the writer to dream up more items than a magazine would ordinarily use. This gives the editor a choice and the script can easily be cut (without hurting the piece *or* the writer) to fit a niche on a page which couldn't accommodate a tightly-written essay. It might even be split into two parts and run in successive issues.

There was a vogue, many years ago, for the surprise-ending technique, the function of which was to upset the premise the writer led the reader to build up. You remember: "He stroked her long, silky hair and whispered, 'I love you, Geraldine.'" This went on for 300 words until we reached the snapper: The subject was a pet cat. It's difficult to fool today's readers, but it can be done. Here are two that did the trick.

THRIFT NOTE

Each night, empty your pocket or purse of pennies and drop them into an old fish tank or unused umbrella stand.

Ask your bank for a supply of paper tubes designed to hold a roll of 50 pennies each. Deposit these rolls in a savings account from time to time.

Within a few months, you'll realize that this accumulation of odd coins won't amount to anything for years.

RECIPE

Flagging appetite? Try this. Over a hot (not flaming) charcoal fire, broil a thick slab of prime sirloin of beef for three and a half minutes. Dice and place in dog's dish. If he still won't eat, take him to a vet.

New forms for short humor are welcomed by the markets. This is one field in which the writer can experiment with impunity. As an editor, I search eagerly for original presentations; and as a writer, I twist and torture my mind, constantly seeking fresh ways to express an amusing notion. Incidentally, if you're aiming at the top markets, don't ever end a piece with the old easy-out line that reads something like this: "Why are you looking so funny, dear? Put down that crowbar! I. . . . Glmmmmmmpf!" This will almost certainly put the kiss of rejection on it.

Lastly, a piece of humor, no matter how short, should be worked over carefully and thoroughly. Its brevity does not condone haste or carelessness. Restrain that impulse to send everything off at once to a publisher. Write and re-write, polish and repolish; then put your brain child away for a few days. When you read it again with a fresh eye, is it still warm, still funny? If it isn't, and it won't respond to further rewriting, throw it away. Short humor is about the most expendable of literary properties; and while pride of authorship is commendable, a feeling that every composition is too precious to cast aside is a great handicap in the creative process.

Joseph Wood Krutch, former professor of Dramatic Literature at Columbia University has said: "Anyone who undertakes to write about how one should write is sticking his neck out."

There's mine.

ROBERT FONTAINE *has written hundreds of radio dramas, essays, humorous pieces for* The Saturday Evening Post *and other magazines, three books, and many poems. His short stories have been published in* The Atlantic Monthly, Redbook, Mademoiselle, Esquire, The Yale Review, The Prairie Schooner, *and several other magazines. His best-selling novel,* The Happy Time, *was successfully adapted for Broadway and the movies.*

VI

HOW TO BE EXCRUCIATINGLY FUNNY IN SHORTS

BY ROBERT FONTAINE

The editor of this tutti-frutti collection has approached me sideways and offered me a controlling interest in the Suez Canal if I will reveal my methods of writing humorous shorts. I have agreed to the offer, but I must explain to the reader that I am not really completely aware of how I do it myself. On the other hand, I have always had one eye on the Suez Canal.

Let me say, by way of preface, that there is not much difference between writing funny short pieces and funny long pieces. The short pieces are usually not quite as long. A short funny piece may be made into a longer one by inserting a few more typewritten pages under the paper clip.

Furthermore, not everybody laughs at funny pieces.

Most editors, for example, never laugh at funny pieces. They have seen so many of mine that if they were to let themselves go they would be just plain worn out. What an editor does when he reads something funny is sort of twitch on one side, scrape his throat, wrinkle up his nose and give an abortive sneeze. It gives the general impression he is suffering from a rare tropical tic picked up while trying to talk an Andaman Islander Shaman into ghosting an article on his tribe's puberty rites.

I should make an exception here. I know one or two editors who *say* they laugh at my comical pieces. I have before me notes like this: "I and the whole staff are still rocking with laughter over the piece on meat loaves you sent us. It certainly brightened up our day and no one knows how much I regret it isn't possible to buy it. Do try us again." (That'll be the day!)

Sometimes I get a picture, from reading these notes, that a few unbridled editors are running a shop where all the staff from the charwoman up are so busted up with laughter after reading my shorts that they can barely stuff the things in return envelopes.

What I am trying to say, seriously, is that nobody knows what a funny short piece is. We all know what a short piece is, but "funny" is something else again. In my youth when I wore bangs and played the flute and was dreadfully naive, I used to try to figure out what *other* people would think was funny. This never worked either, so I reverted to the "Big I" system or "What I think is funny is funny and any editor who doesn't agree, may his newsstand sales drop twenty-two per-cent in Kenosha!" This also doesn't work, but it makes me feel better because if nobody in the business laughs at some of my things, you can bet that I do. Anyone who reads a short piece of mine in some journal and thinks, "This isn't a bit funny," might like to know I laughed myself sidesaddle writing it. My wife and family also laughed at it or they didn't get any dinner that night.

In all sweet solemnity, there is one nice thing about making up short funnies. If no one ever buys them you have a lot of droll remarks to make at parties. What's more, short humor is the only thing I write that I thoroughly enjoy, and if anybody wants to give me money for it, it's like velvet blankets over silk sheets—so much the better.

Well, here I am rambling on about myself and not a word about you. You want, I suppose, to know how I go about plying my trade. First, I do a lot of thinking. I do this mostly when there is no one home because I find it trying to think when anyone is in the house. As I sit there thinking, I am often struck with a hilarious idea. I double up with laughter that resounds through the vacant rooms. I roll on the floor, banging my fists on my chest, kicking my feet about and often fracturing a toe. (I always try to think barefoot.)

When this subsides, I make my way upstairs to my study where I put one side of a white sheet of paper in my typewriter and then I forget what I was laughing about.

The average writer would go out and get drunk at this point. If he were more seasoned, he would stay home and get drunk. I do neither. I sit there and stare. After a while there slowly oozes up through the subconscious an idea that turns left at the occiput, takes the elevator to the midbrain and then springs out at me in full bloom.

At this point the telephone rings and a man wants to know if I have his shoes half-soled yet.

If you want to find out who is a writer of short humorous pieces you need only find a character whose telephone rings when he starts to work. If he has an earth-shakingly funny idea, the telephone is long distance from New York and consists of a hot tip on a Canadian oil stock that will triple your money in three weeks. Will he put aside 5000 shares for you? No, he won't.

There is one more sign of the true humorous writer and that is that he has an intercom in his study and when he is doubled up with a great notion, his wife calls him on the intercom and wants to know if he has enough wool socks up there.

After all this is gone through, the writer takes the blank sheet out of the typewriter and puts in another one. The first one he would never again use. It is covered with wet tears, and anyway it is now totem. (Cf. Malinowski: *The Sexual Life of the Savages*)

If he is lucky and the rain doesn't beat down too hard on the roof and the doves don't coo too loud and the barometric pressure is right and the temperature is normal, the writer usually thinks of something amusing to write.

I hear you asking, "Where do you find the funny things to write?" This question often occurs to me so I have taken down from my valuable library a copy of a collection of "Postscripts" from *The Saturday Evening Post* in which I appear a number of times. Not often enough, maybe, but plenty.

The first piece I see by me is called "Letter from Camp" and that is just what it is: a letter from my oldest daughter in summer camp. I don't think I changed more than a dozen words, simply eliminating profanity and such. She was nine years old at the time and was developing the wrong type of vocabulary. Anyway, this piece ends, "We are studying crafts and Ferna started to make a bead bag but she is trying it on her feet now and maybe it will be a hat."

So there is one way to find funny pieces.

The next piece I see is "I Shall Have Music." This is devoted to an analysis of how it takes me three hours to play Chopin's "Minute Waltz" properly. (But when *I* get finished with it, it's *done!*) "Every note I play is clear and isolated. Lonely even." Well, this struck me as a funny notion because it is exactly how I *do* play the piano. I can read music, but I'm in no hurry to do it. I can read the various marks but it takes me a little time to do anything about it. I really enjoy playing the piano that way. For a long time it never struck me funny. Then one day it did. I wrote the piece. So one way to write a funny piece is to observe yourself carefully and see if there aren't some odd ways you have of doing things. My wife, for example, sticks her tongue way out and moves it in a semicircle when she's sewing. It looks very funny. I think she'd move it in a complete circle if it had ball bearings. Someday I'll write something funny about that.

The next piece in this volume of "Postscripts" is "How To Finish a Table." This was at the height of the do-it-yourself craze, and I tried to take the finish off a table and put another one on. I am the world's worst do-it-yourself-er. In fact, I usually can't even find anyone to do it *for* me. Anyway, this piece told how I finished a table, and it ended up with my taking an axe and chopping it up. Then it was finished.

The next piece was called "Letter from a Fairly Unknown Woman" and again was a slightly edited note from one of my daughters announcing that she had decided to be a fashion model and was changing her name and would we please send her some high heels and a lipstick.

Another piece called "The Jolly Painters" described almost accurately my adventures while having three artistic characters, union members all, paint the interior of my house. It was all quite a mess. The painters were very sensitive and got three dollars an hour explaining how sensitive they were, while the boss got four dollars an hour flirting with my wife. I got back at them all with this little piece. Revenge is especially sweet when you get money for it.

Still another piece has to do with my reactions to a symphony concert. My wife used to insist on dragging me to concerts, which I abhor. I don't mind classical music in my own home where I can sleep comfortably, but public concerts upset me and give me a crick in the neck. I said as much in this piece and when my wife read it she turned red and never made me go to a concert again.

There is a piece here called "Household Hints." My wife went away to chaperone a beach week for my daughters' sorority and I was left all alone with the dishes. The result was quite an experience, which I later passed on to other lonely husbands. A couple of the hints are as follows and they are worth their weight in gold:

> Shorts and undershirts, after being washed, may be dried quickly by putting them on and going for a walk. They do not need to be ironed unless you are expecting the doctor.

> Wastebaskets can be used much longer if you get in them and jump up and down every day.

> If you do not put enough water in the rice when cooking it, you will have something else for dinner.

These, obviously, are funny because they are all too sadly true.

The final short by me in this volume is "What Ever Happened to Fathers?" My experience as a father was beginning to tell on me and I compared the days when I was a kid and my father was boss, to the days when I was the father and I had to get up and give the kids the comfortable chair. It seemed unfair. It still does.

Maybe all these things did not reduce you to fits of laughter. That is because everyone does not laugh at the same things. This is what you are up against in writing humor for magazines.

I used to write for radio and TV comedians, and when you write for them you normally do not have to worry about the audience laughing. You just spell out the joke in big letters for the comic to say and he says it. After that you write, (LAUGHTER). This means the audience laughs. A big neon sign lights up and says, LAUGH. If you don't, some of the younger men from the advertising agency walk through the aisles and horsewhip you. If you are an outstanding offender you may be banished from TV audiences forever. In that tribe, it is tantamount to death.

Of course, if you are at home listening or viewing and you don't think something is funny you may write a letter to the station. This will do you no good because all letters are in the charge of chimpanzees, and the odds are astronomical against one of them even addressing an envelope properly.

On the other hand, when you write for a magazine there is no one to beat the reader into submission. He reads your piece, and if he doesn't chuckle you're sunk. You can't flash lights in front of him or explain to him or try something else.

All right, suppose we try to put down some easy-to-remember rules about writing short humor. First, though, let us list possible places to find ideas.

1. *Serious Magazine Articles.* Magazines these days are all full of malarkey about how to be beautiful, how to get

rich, how to be nervous, how to build your own scaffold and all that stuff. Sometimes just reading an article like that aloud makes you laugh, and you can see that a little distortion here and there would make a funny piece. I once read an article by Marilyn Monroe on "How I Keep Beautiful." I wrote an article on how *I* keep beautiful. I used almost the same ideas as Monroe only on me they looked funny because while we both have the same measurements we have them in different places.

2. *The Inverted Idea.* This follows from #1. You read an article or piece about how to be rich or how to diet and then you invert it. You do something about how to be poor or how to get fat. Or, you turn the thing inside out. For example, while I have been sitting here doing nothing, I have been making notes for a piece about diets for, say, *Playboy.* This will consist of several diets for he-men and philanderers. What about a liquid diet consisting entirely of Scotch? People should eat stretched out flat so the food can disperse to the ends instead of settling in the middle. And so on.

3. *The Personal Problem.* All of us have problems of love, home, family and parental duty. They are serious problems, but when one of them is settled, it is well to look back in laughter. I have often left a bitter quarrel with my wife, walked upstairs with a piece of beefsteak to my eye, and then begun to see the humorous side of the thing. I recall once being able to get a piece out of it on "How To Understand What a Woman Is Talking About." I also did another called, "You Keep Talking But What Are You Saying?" It is best not to show these pieces to your wife.

My children have also suggested funny articles. Recently,

I had a letter from my daughter in college complaining about the food, the strict housemother, the lack of boys, and so on. I wrote *her* a letter complaining about the food at home, the strict wife, the lack of well-stacked chicks, and the way all the other fathers had Jaguars and I had a 1953 Hudson Jet. The letter, with some minor editing, made a good little piece.

4. *The Academic Drivel.* I usually write these shorts after reading a long, tiresome book on psychoanalysis, anthropology or economics. The gag here is to use the vocabulary and attitude of scholars in writing about commonplace affairs. I did a successful article on a feud with my neighbor, couching it in terms of diplomatic notes and foreign affairs commentators. I have often done pieces about weddings, birthday parties, and love affairs from the standpoint of an anthropologist. Psychotherapy offers many opportunities of explaining obvious things in a funny way by getting involved as hell with Freudian jargon.

5. *The Burlesque.* Exaggeration of solemn attitudes to the point of absurdity causes burlesque. An example was an article I wrote called, "I Was A Teen-Age Werewolf in Cairo's Sexy Alleys!" This was a gross parody of all the he-man stories about white slavery, hand-to-hand combats with sharks, army ants, Mau Mau rites and heaven knows what else.

6. *Statistics.* We live by statistics. You can hardly open a newspaper without reading that 11% of the American people sleep with one foot on the floor; that ten years after graduation the average Yale man has 1½ children. Statistics are absurd because they never provide the truth about anything, and yet they claim to. The death rate of kangaroos is almost on the same curve with the increase in

cigarette smoking in America. Are we permitting kangaroos to smoke too many cigarettes? It is an easy trick to take
up some set of statistics and draw valid but nonsensical
conclusions from them.

7. *Irrelevancies.* You can think these up by yourself. It is
only necessary to start an apparently serious essay and then
go wandering off in all directions. "How About Our Policy
in Utria?" might be a good title, and then go on to invent
authorities who claim we are shipping too many bolts to
Utria, providing an imbalance of nuts thus lowering the
output of ingots, and so on.

8. *Modern Complexities.* Great fun can be had from the
fact that man has swept ahead scientifically a lot faster than
he has intellectually. The result is he is a neurotic child
playing with baffling toys he made with his own Meccano
Set #7. I recall a piece of mine about secretarial machines
that took dictation directly on the typewriter from sound
vibrations of the human voice. What I was working on was
an attachment that would make it giggle and allow itself to
be chased around an office desk.

There are the vending machines that, when you want
hot coffee, give your feet a massage. There are space rockets
that have gone down instead of up, making a hell of a hole
in the ground. There was the first dog in an artificial
satellite that kept sending back "Bow-wow" in Morse code.
There was the mouse that went up and sent back
"Meeow!", baffling everybody.

There are all the gimmicks around the house that per-
mit the homemaker long hours of leisure in which to see
her psychiatrist. There are hubby's power tools which take
on a life of their own and cut the legs off the table on
which they are mounted. Modern life knows no limit to

the number of comforting life-saving devices that are killing us. They cry out for humorous treatment.

There are hundreds of other divisions into which material for short pieces might fall. I have merely listed a few that came to mind as I was standing here in the cold shower. By pasting this book in your hat, you'll have a handy reference when you are stuck for something humorous to write about.

I suppose a lot of you are saying, "That's all very well, but we don't even know how to type up short pieces or how to mail them or anything. Shucks!"

Well, I'm going to make a brief list of the items that might confuse you along those lines and see if we can't get all confused together.

1. Write on one side of the paper. A lot of people want to write on two sides of the paper because there *are* two sides to the paper. This seems logical but it isn't. Take my word for it.

2. Use white bond paper about 16-lb weight. I don't know what 16-lb weight means either, but it means that paper is what you may use. Some people, especially women, use lavender or pink paper. This gives male editors the idea you are saying something seductive between the lines. And you know how male editors are, don't you?

3. Enclose a self-addressed stamped envelope. The envelope you enclose should be large enough to put the manuscript in. If you enclose a self-addressed stamped envelope the editor will see you are modest enough not to be sure your ms. will be accepted. Editors like modest writers. They usually are willing to accept the minimum rate until they're ready for social security.

4. Whom should you address short pieces to? This has puzzled me for some time. I started out addressing: Short Feature Editor. The first feature editor I met was nine feet tall so I saw my error. Then I said, "Editor Shorts." They had no editor named Shorts. The closest they could come was Hibbs and that isn't very close. I finally chose "Editorial Department: Short Features." This seems to work except that the rejections often come back with a note signed by Rose Framingpaugh, Associate Nylon Hose Editor. I remember, and this is a fact, a short feature I addressed to the editor of *Esquire* many years ago. He wrote me in person that somehow or other he was afraid the charwoman had thrown the piece in the wastebasket, but they were going to reject it anyway. This was the oddest rejection I ever had but one. That was when the charwoman sent me back the piece and said she didn't think it was funny, would I try again.

5. How long should a short piece be? Well, short humorous pieces run from 150 words to maybe 500. Pieces of a thousand words are still short pieces, but they will have to be fairly brilliant to sell. It is awfully hard to be funny for more than five hundred words, as readers of this unlimited chapter have probably noticed. Pieces over a thousand words should be called "light-hearted," because what you have to do there is take a light-hearted approach to some serious matter. You can be mildly humorous but you can't use burlesque or satire or irony.

6. How many short pieces should you submit at once? That depends. No editor likes to get so many pieces from one writer at once that he can't lift them. Editors often judge manuscripts by weight, so be wary.

Finally, let me tell you all how I got started being a humorist. I do it because it seems to me a good way to have fun, to develop your style, and to find out something about your audience.

I began by writing letters to local newspapers. I tried to be funny in those letters. I took local or national happenings, and I wrote tongue-in-cheek letters about them. This started other people answering my letters in print, and it began friendships with a number of neighbors and fellow citizens who would say, "That was a very funny letter you had in the paper today." Or, "I didn't think that last letter of yours was as funny as the first two." In this way I began to be able to judge what my contemporaries thought amusing and what they didn't think amusing. It was awfully good training and, as I said, a lot of fun. I branched out after that and wrote letters to the New York and Boston papers, and this was good training, too. Eventually an editor wrote me, "Why don't you try some of your humorous stuff on the magazines?" That was all I needed!

In fact, even today I cannot always resist the temptation to sound off absurdly about some event in town. Recently, and in the midst of the President's "Buy Now" campaign, several successful opium pushers were arrested. I wrote quite an indignant letter to the paper; something like this:

Gentlemen:
   I read of the arrest of Big Head Sam and Little Feet McGinnis with some regret. It seems to me that now, when the President is urging us to buy to keep the economy healthy, we should salute those who are pushing their goods rather than restrain them.
   Think of the chain of events here. Big Head Sam gets a new car every year with his profits. This means work in Detroit. It means the steel furnaces are glowing. It means

the stock market is rising. If the police are going to clamp down on every small businessman, we are in for a state of monopoly. And if the dope pushers are busted, what is the next step? Obviously, there will be a crackdown on the bookies, and we all know what unhappiness that will cause the average citizen like me.

Furthermore, it appears to me that if we are going to jail men like Big Head where is the workingman going to get his opium? Many workers are unemployed. They are nervous and at loose ends. They look forward to their pipe at the end of the day.

I have been told by Nice Nellies that opium is bad for the health. This is hard to believe. If the workingman can't get his opium he will turn to cigarettes. As we all know, cigarettes cause lung cancer. There is no known case of opium causing lung cancer.

Finally, let us use the police for what they were intended: that is, to stop all that necking in Forest Park. That's where they're needed!

> Yours truly,
> Yung Hung Fing
> Loyal Citizen

If you have any sort of a sense of humor, you can rattle off this sort of stuff by the yard. Newspapers are always amused by it, because it prompts further letters and debates and brightens up the city editor's day. Of course, you won't make any money this way, but you'll learn your craft and get to know what makes people laugh.

And that is about all I have to say this evening. In fact I don't know why I should encourage competition. I'm having a hard enough time as it is. Frankly I don't quite know how I got into this. I don't want the Suez Canal *that* badly!

DAN BENNETT, *a* nom de plume *for Ben Cassell, has been writing humor since 1944, when a severe illness forced him to forego a career as chief engineer with one of the world's largest construction companies. For several years he wrote comedy for Bob Burns, Jimmy Durante and other comedians in radio and television. At present, he directs the activities of two of his own television shows and writes humor in his spare time.*

VII

WRITING THE SHORT HUMOR ITEM

BY DAN BENNETT

A Short Humor Item Do-It-Yourself Writing Kit consists of the following:

1 typewriter
1 table
1 chair
1 supply of paper and carbon
1 supply of envelopes and stamps
1 average I.Q.
1 superlative of stubbornness and perseverance

Humor is a personal thing—different to each person—and the art of writing humor is not learned from a book. What *can* be learned from a book is the form to use to send humor to the market place, ideas about where to get ideas, the compilation of material, slanting for specific markets, selling the manuscript and, most important of all, the market place itself.

Since I would not presume to give instruction in the art of writing humor, what I can do is tell others how I write myself, in the hope that my methods and experience might be of some benefit. But in the final analysis, each person who writes any type of literary material at all must work out his own salvation. There are no magic formulae. *You have to do the creating and writing yourself!* Nobody can tell you how!

In the science of General Semantics, originated by the Polish engineer, Alfred Korzybski, there is a phrase used frequently: "inside your skin." Applied to the creation of humor, I take it to mean that many writers get only a surface appreciation or surface feeling of the humor involved when they write, and they do not concentrate on the subject enough; or they are not sufficiently interested to work and study to get the necessary feeling or understanding of the humor of a written line. Thus they cannot tell if something is funny or not.

By concentrating and studying humor over a period of time, all writers who are successful in this field come to have that unconscious "inside your skin" feeling. Humor writers who have acquired the necessary experience can look at a line and tell immediately if it has a chance or not. And, as far as the ultimate sale is concerned, they are right far more often than they are wrong. They don't have to stop and classify the humor as 1) a Silly Situation, 2) a Reverse, 3) a Cliché, 4) a Well-Known Expression, or one of the other countless classifications that some instructors apply to humor. Because they have a deep "inside the skin" feeling of humor, they know immediately if it is good or not. The mechanical process of classifying does not lend itself to the creative arts, especially during the period of creation. And since this "inside the skin" knowledge can be gained only by long study of what has been done in the field of humor, what is being done, and by actually doing it yourself, it follows that the compilation of material is important.

The short humor forms that I specialize in are the Epigram, the Anecdote, and the Cartoon Gag. Before each type is analyzed, here are some things that apply in general to all three types.

THE COMPILATION OF MATERIAL

Every writer of the short humor item should have a file of humorous material to use as a springboard for new ideas. This means saving and putting into a usable file any humor material that he feels will be helpful in his work. This might include published epigrams, jokes, anecdotes, light verse, magazine cartoons, comic strips, amusing essays, collections of jokes and gags, funny true experiences, or old magazines and books containing humor items. I like to save the humor pages from magazines, and when I get enough of them, have them bound with a hard cover, labeled on the outside as to contents. I then place them in my library for reference. I also use scrapbooks for filing short items such as epigrams and poetry. I am constantly on the lookout for old humor books and magazines because they are the best source for new ideas that I know of. Also, they are invaluable for study of types and techniques of humor written in the past.

A good file takes a lot of room, and material for it must be saved over the years to be of any value. Classify your material in the way that you can use it best. Each writer has a different technique and therefore each uses his file in a different manner. But keep a file!

THE MARKET PLACE

Writers very seldom write for their own amusement. They write for one thing—money! And the money is in the markets and has to be pried loose. So it follows that, other things being equal, the writer who knows the most about the markets for his particular type of writing is the most successful.

For many years I have taken every writers' magazine that is published, for one purpose—the hope of picking up even one additional market for my writing. It is surprising how a relatively small and unknown market, found in an obscure listing, can be developed into a source of steady income because it is not well enough known to have too many submissions of material.

Each market should be studied carefully for its editorial policy. Get back copies of the magazines and study the type of humor they print, and soon a common denominator will emerge. Perhaps it's a family magazine which likes an anecdote or epigram that appeals to everyone in the family group. A man's magazine is not going to be interested in the bright sayings of children, but in something a lot more earthy. A woman's magazine is more interested in problems that confront women than in gags about sports and gambling. If submissions are made to a particular market without regard to its wants, the whole thing becomes a waste of the writer's time and money. *Learn the markets—and give each magazine the type of material it wants.*

Markets can also be created. There are thousands upon thousands of trade magazines and house organs in the

United States. The trade magazine is published for the benefit of people working in a certain industry, such as insurance, groceries, etc. The house organ is a magazine published by a certain company to keep its employees informed of what is going on in the company, and some of these magazines use humor to break the monotony of their publications. A humor writer who is on his toes can convince an editor who uses no humor that he may gain reader interest by including a quarter, a half or even a full page of humor. Naturally this takes a sales campaign, but if the editor agrees to let the writer furnish all the humor, it's a campaign won.

There are also thousands of weekly newspapers in America that are potential customers for the short humor item. One writer I know secured a "chain" of twenty small-town newspapers as markets to whom he sold a quarter-page weekly humor column. Heaven knows how many letters he wrote, how many different small-town newspapers he approached, before developing that particular market for his wares.

Another thing that must be remembered is that the bigger the magazine, the more competition there will be from other writers. A beginning writer can protect his ego by submitting his material to smaller markets, with much more chance of success until he learns the ropes. In the main, manuscripts can sell only at their own level, and most writers are slow to learn, and often unwilling to believe, what that level actually is.

An experienced writer gets to the point where he will not consider writing any item that will not fit into one or more of his regular market categories.

There is no absolute gauge or guide. In a way, finding a place for what one writes is not unlike finding a job. It takes a lot of hunting around, and not infrequently takes a lot of luck as well, but in the long run, as we know, most people do find jobs.

THE EPIGRAM

An epigram is a grain of truth told in the twinkling of an eye. The epigram is a short idea, the distillation of many words and thoughts. A person doesn't have to read 5,000 words to arrive at the conclusion an epigram brings him to immediately. For instance:

"Times have changed. Our fathers and grandfathers never dreamed of getting anything more from the government than a few garden seeds." A few words tell the whole story. This short epigram spans three generations and brings to mind a myriad of thoughts, different to each reader.

Take this one: "A bachelor is a man who can put on his socks from either end." This epigram conjures up an immediate humorous picture, as well as many other ideas about bachelors. It acts as a springboard to "A bachelor is a man who can't put something down in his apartment without putting it down on something else," or "A bachelor is a man who has to know how to remove a coffee stain from a catsup stain from a white tablecloth."

One thought leads to another, and one epigram also leads to another. An epigram can be a play on words, a pun perhaps, if it's good enough, but since the epigram is concerned with words, the epigram writer should become word-conscious. He should enlarge his vocabulary by studying the dictionary. He should carry a notebook and pencil and write down words or combinations of words he hears that appeal to his sense of humor. He should read and read and read—anything he can lay his hands on—because he never knows where an idea for an epigram will come from.

When it comes to the form to use for sending the epigram to the market place, there is no standard. I cut a sheet of 8½ by 11 paper into strips 8½ inches wide and about 2 inches deep. In the upper left-hand corner goes my name and address, in the upper right-hand corner goes my file number, leaving enough room on the strip for the typing of one epigram up to three lines in length. Naturally all epigrams should be typed and a carbon copy kept for the writer's file.

There have always been a lot of arguments as to how many epigrams should go to an editor in one batch. I take the position that quality pays off more than quantity. I write my epigrams in longhand one week and type them the following week, thus giving them a chance to cool off in the interim. It's surprising how many that looked good when I wrote them don't look so good a week later. Thus, by throwing out the ones I don't think will have a chance, I manage to come up with ten epigrams for a batch, which I type and send out. Ten epigrams, together with the forwarding envelope and the self-addressed, stamped return envelope, will go through the mails for a 4¢ stamp, with no overdue postage problem.

On the back of each carbon of the batch of epigrams, I stamp the date it goes out and write the name of the magazine to which it is sent. If one epigram is held by a magazine for further consideration, a notation is made on the back of the carbon copy. If the epigram is sold, the date sold and the price paid go on the back of the copy before it is placed in my "Sold" file. In other words, the back of the carbon copy of each epigram carries the whole history of that particular epigram. If one is held and then rejected,

I note this on the back of the copy because it might be possible to interest that same market a following year.

Nobody can tell you how to write an epigram. You have to write it yourself. Take some famous old proverbs and try to twist them around to come up with something funny or philosophical. Take some old clichés, some well-known expressions, some wisecracks, and play around with the wording. Add some new words, substitute other words, shorten or lengthen. Practice! Write! Study! The popularity of the epigram is increasing all the time and writing them pays off.

THE ANECDOTE

The anecdote is a humorous story of an incident, which means anything from a two-line joke up to a story of a thousand words. Study the markets, pay attention to the anecdotal word requirements of the various magazines.

The origins of the anecdotes which are published in leading magazines today are very obscure. Many of those which are printed regularly are merely old jokes, brought up-to-date by the inclusion of modern implements. Others are true happenings, made more palatable by some polishing of the punch-lines. Still others are vignettes which have a particular point to make.

Most magazines want anecdotes about people and everyday life that are funny and point up a certain moral. They aim for identification with their readers, which every branch of entertainment and publishing seems to think is important in this modern age. However, some magazines lean toward the screwball type of anecdote which is a fantasy of the imagination, the type of thing that is funny but could never happen.

Again, as in the case of the epigram, the only way to

satisfy the markets is to study them carefully. Current and back copies of magazines show the type of humor they buy.

There is no standard form for sending the anecdote to an editor. I cut an 8½ by 11 piece of paper into two pieces 8½ by 5½. Name and address go in the upper left-hand corner, of course. I try to limit the length of my anecdotes to about 150 or 160 words, which will go comfortably on an 8½ by 5½ piece of paper. I send my anecdotes to market six in a batch, and including the forwarding and return envelope, they will travel for 4¢ without an overweight problem. As in the case with epigrams, on the back of the carbon copy of the anecdote go the date it goes to market, the market's name and any other pertinent information.

Anecdotes are created in several ways. They can be switched from other jokes, which is the most common way. They can be built backwards from a funny punch-line; they can be built on a true happening; and they can be created out of thin air by a good imagination. Again comes the reason for keeping a good file of jokes, epigrams, cartoons and anything else that's funny. Reading humor is one of the best ways to get ideas for new humor. Keeping your eyes open for funny situations in real life is a must, for the humorist has to be observant and see the humor in situations around him.

And when you sit down to write the anecdote, know your markets well enough so that you can slant your material to their wants.

THE CARTOON GAG

Everyone is familiar with the magazine cartoon gag that is so popular these days. But maybe everyone doesn't know that most of the cartoon gags are originated by cartoon gagwriters, sent to the cartoonist who picks the ones he wants, draws them up, sells them and then gives the cartoon gagwriter a percentage of the selling price of the cartoon. This percentage is never lower than 25% and can go as high as the individual deal makes it.

I divide all cartoon gags into three categories:

(1) The Literary Cartoon: A funny caption attached to a drawing with no action in it. The drawing is usually a couple of people talking, and the caption would stand by itself without the drawing.

(2) The Captionless Cartoon: The funny drawing which needs no caption to explain it. The whole meaning is in the drawing.

(3) The Blend: The cartoon adds something to the caption, and the caption adds something to the cartoon. This is the perfect magazine cartoon.

Naturally the latter two types are the most popular and the ones most in demand by cartoonists. There's a special form in which to send out cartoon gags.

They should be typed on 3″ by 5″ cards, with a carbon copy kept for the writer's file. In the upper left-hand corner of the card goes the writer's name and address. In the upper right-hand corner goes the writer's file number for the gag. Then comes the Scene and Caption, so the submission looks like this:

Dan Bennett   #3789
1111 Smith Road
Los Angeles, Calif.

SCENE: Mother talks to another woman as her little boy stands nearby with extremely long hair.

CAPTION: "Junior's growing Mother a switch, aren't you, darling?"

The names and addresses of cartoonists wanting gags from gagwriters can be obtained from Earle Tempel, P. O. Box 430, Van Buren, Arkansas, who publishes several magazines about cartooning and gagwriting. You can also write to the cartoonist in care of any magazine in which his work appears and make arrangements with him.

Six 3″ by 5″ cards with gags on them can be sent out to the cartoonist in one batch, plus the self-addressed, stamped return envelope. A good thing to remember is that most of the leading cartoonists get hundreds of gags in the mail every day, and they don't like to read through a lot of junk. Keep your batches short and your gags good.

The biggest complaint that cartoonists have with beginning gagwriters is that all of their gags are old and have been done. A thorough study has to be made by the beginner of everything that's been done in the cartoon field so he won't repeat published gags. It follows that a file of old cartoons is a must, both for study and as a base or springboard to new ideas.

Cartoon gags should always be kept simple, with a minimum of characters in the drawing and a minimum of dialogue in the caption.

HINTS TO THE WISE

Always use a self-addressed, stamped envelope if you want to get your material back from either an editor or cartoonist. Always put your name and address on each piece of material. Always type everything you send out.

*   *   *

Keep your items as short as you can. That's the way to make them sparkle.

*   *   *

Avoid anything repulsive or disgusting.

*   *   *

Never use swear words.

*   *   *

Never use anything offensive to any race, religion or color.

*   *   *

Keep your manuscripts clean and presentable. Retype them if they come back dog-eared or ragged.

*   *   *

When you once write something, send it out and forget about it, and concentrate on writing something else. Keep your items on the road. They don't have a chance of selling while lying in a desk drawer or in a filing cabinet.

*   *   *

Never throw away anything you have written and not sold. Put it away in your slush pile and when you get time, take it out and rework it into something salable. Times and editors change, and what isn't funny to them one year might be the next.

*   *   *

Don't get discouraged if you keep seeing the same names in magazines all the time. There is plenty of room for you. The reason the same names appear constantly is that those are the writers who have stuck with it—writing and learning as they go along. Remember, editors will buy anything if it's good enough.

*   *   *

Don't worry about magazines stealing your writing and then not paying you for it. Magazines will lean over backwards to be fair with you. They pay for what they use.

*   *   *

The best way to write humor is to have a steady job from which you derive an income. In your spare time you can free lance in the humor field until you are well launched. Then, and only then, is it advisable to relinquish your position.

*   *   *

There is no rule or law that will make you a writer of truly funny humor. A successful humorist must have a natural knack for humor and acquire technique through experience.

VIII

LIGHT VERSE MUST BE THE RIGHT VERSE

By Richard Armour

To the unpracticed eye, the difference between slightly amusing doggerel and brightly amusing light verse is only paper thin. But, thin as it is, the paper is a check, "And, oh, the difference to me!" in the words of Wordsworth, who was not a light verse writer but a heavy verse writer. Also Wordsworth was writing about the death of Lucy, which is not the sort of thing you would write lightly about.

The trouble with light verse is that almost anyone can write it, but only a few can write it well enough to get editors to buy it and readers to read it. To the extent that writing light verse depends on a special attitude toward life, a turn of mind, it cannot be learned by reading about it. To the extent, however, that it depends on skill, a turn of phrase, it can indeed be learned. Great (or at least competent) writers from little aptitudes grow. Like poets, light verse writers are born—and made better.

This brings up the question about whether light verse is poetry. I would say that it is at least a relative, a Cinderella sister, and it uses most of the techniques and devices of poetry, such as rhyme and meter and alliteration and imagery and the nuances of sound. The aim of light verse is not so high as that of poetry, and a great piece of light verse is not on the same level as a great poem. I find it easier and less pretentious to call myself a light verse writer rather than a poet. Someone has said that to call oneself a poet takes the bravery of a man facing a wild bull with a sharpened lead pencil.

A bad poem, because of what it has striven in vain to be, is a more dismal thing than a bad piece of light verse. Sometimes you can get humor by purposely writing bad poetry, as Ogden Nash has done. But Nash has accomplished more than this, with his limping meters and wild rhymes. He has parodied poetry, especially the sentimental poems of the nineteenth century, and he has invariably had something of his own to say, as he turned bad poetry into good light verse. Let Ogden Nash alone. Do not try to imitate him. He has developed something that bears his trademark. If you want to imitate someone, and I believe in imitation as one of the best ways of learning anything, whether it is playing tennis or tooting a flute, study the more traditional and orthodox light verse writers, like Arthur Guiterman, Samuel Hoffenstein, Dorothy Parker, Margaret Fishback, David McCord, Morris Bishop, and Phyllis McGinley.

To define light verse, I would call it "poetry written in the spirit of play" or "humor in verse." It eschews the lofty thoughts, strong emotions, and beautiful imagery of poetry and instead goes in for absurdity, ridicule, and technical virtuosity. Light verse is rarely written with any success in blank verse or free verse forms. On the contrary, it emphasizes rollicking meters, odd and unexpected rhymes, and novel arrangements of lines and stanzas, along with word play and double meaning.

Let me now make a few specific points about light verse. First, it is usually short—as short as the couplet, and seldom over sixteen lines. The couplet, the quatrain, the eight-liner are most in demand in magazines as fillers, for they fill out a column where the prose does not quite reach the bottom of the page, and they are as useful as a cartoon or a quip to break up the monotony of a solid page of prose. Besides, they can be read quickly as the reader flips through. Here are a few of my own short pieces, couplets and quatrains, with comments.

Inscription for a Fly Swatter

The hand is quicker than the eye is,
But somewhat slower than the fly is.

This one, quite obviously, deals with an experience with which everyone is familiar. It is something the reader will understand at first reading. Readers of serious poetry, especially in a required course in school, will read a poem over and over to get the meaning. But not the reader of light verse. Yet the piece should be a bit out of the ordinary, the reader should simultaneously smile at the idea and appreciate the unusual way the idea is stated. Here there are two tricks that perhaps lifted the couplet into the selling bracket: (1) play with the familiar saying, "The hand is quicker than the eye," and (2) the double rhyme of "eye is" and "fly is."

Or look at another:

Lady Shoppers, Beware

Show-window manikins
Have slenderer fannykins.

This time the idea, a commentary on the way of almost all flesh, is commonplace again, sadly commonplace. If you were to say, "Women shoppers have bigger behinds than do clothes models in windows," it would be merely a statement of fact and not the least funny. But in this piece of verse the three-syllable rhyme of "manikins" and "fannykins" made it a sale to *Collier's.*

I remember another occasion when the unusual triple rhyme was all there was to it, in a couplet in *The New Yorker* which went:

> With girls renowned for having glamour a
> Lot depends upon the camera.

One of the shortest pieces I ever wrote (though I once did one for *The Saturday Review* that had no words at all, only punctuation marks) was this one, which gets added fun out of the contrast between an eight-word title and a four-word poem:

Fond Farewell of a Teen-Age Snack Snagger

> See you later,
> Refrigerator.

The idea for this came not only from my forever-nibbling daughter but from the current teen-age expression, "See you later, alligator."

Sometimes it is hard to decide whether to write a piece as a couplet or as a quatrain. This one, called "Middle Age," I might have set down in two lines, but I chose to draw it out into four so that the reader would not get to the end of it quite so fast:

> Middle age
> Is a time of life
> That a man first notices
> In his wife.

I have noticed this reprinted a number of times without the "that" in the third line, and perhaps it is not necessary.

Another one that might just as well have been a couplet is "Going to Extremes":

> Shake and shake
> The catsup bottle.
> None will come,
> And then a lot'll.

My friend David McCord, one of the best of our contemporary light verse writers and the most learned student of this literary form, tells me that he thinks this would be better as a couplet, and he may be right. McCord, by the way, is the editor of what is by far the best collection of humorous verse (at least until he completes his revision of the Carolyn Wells anthology). This is *What Cheer,* which is now available in a Modern Library edition. It is one of the books I keep at my bedside and comb for ideas and inspiration as well as sheer pleasure.

An example of a full-fledged quatrain, which could not be a couplet, is this:

Lady, Your Claws are Showing

> One dreadful truth I rather wish
> I did not know is that
> A woman who is kittenish
> May one day be a cat.

This, I believe, was suggested by Ogden Nash's poem about how sad it is that kittens grow up to be cats. But I gave it a slight twist, playing with the meanings of "kittenish" and "cat" as applied to women. As to form, this is a straightforward a, b, a, b quatrain, smooth and correct, I hope, but with no unusual rhymes. Here the thought and the word play were counted on to do the job.

On the other hand there is this quatrain, in the same general form, in which unusualness of the key rhyme, the rhyme of the second and fourth lines, is essential if the piece is to have enough humorous lift:

On Seeing an X-Ray Picture of Myself

Although I've really never been
  Entranced with my exterior,
I must admit I'm glad for skin,
  My inside's so much eerier.

Sometimes I use the a, b, c, b rhyme form, and do not rhyme the first and third lines, as in the next one:

Would You Mind Taking Your Elbow Out of My Ear?

"Come on," they said, "let's double up
  And all go in our car."
Now we are in, and you should see
  How doubled up we are.

I prefer to rhyme the first and third lines as well as the second and fourth. It is neater and tighter this way, and indicates a little more difficulty overcome. But here it could not be done without spoiling the natural flow. The main thing, anyhow, was that word play with "double up." Moreover, I helped make up for any deficiency, I think, by the rather crazy but appropriate title, and the sum total passed editorial scrutiny at *The Saturday Evening Post*.

Titles, I might add, are of considerable importance in light verse. I would never think of submitting a piece without a title, and I always try to make the title a sort of plus item. Sometimes it helps bring out the point of a poem. Sometimes (as in the long one I cited with the couplet) it is so incongruous as to lend humor. Sometimes it is funny itself. Examples of the latter are titles like "Cats May Have Nine Lives, but I Have Only One" and "Where There's Smoke, There's My Fireplace" and "What You Don't Know Won't Hurt You Till Later." Then there is this one, which needs to be seen with the couplet of which it is a part:

Nip and Tuckered

They say he hits the bottle, and, alack,
The way he looks, the bottle must hit back.

A problem with light verse, as with any form of writing, is how to hold the reader. At least with light verse—if it is properly short—you do not need to hold him quite so long. Catherine Drinker Bowen, the noted biographer, has said that she keeps a large sign on her desk, which she sees every time she looks up from writing. The sign poses this pertinent question: "Will the reader turn the page?" The light verse writer's sign might read: "Will the reader read the next line, the next stanza?"

Ideally, the reader will be held by the humor and the originality of what is being said and by the expectation of what is to come. But one way to hold him, by sheer skill, is with unusual and amusing rhymes, or by playing a kind of rhyme game, in which the reader is curious to see what word you can possibly come up with to rhyme with the word at the end of the line he has just read.

Rhyming can be pointed up and emphasized if the lines are very short and the rhymes, therefore, come close together. Here is an illustration:

Moths

Moths feed
On tweed

And splurge
On serge.

They dote
On coat,

Decant
The pant,

Digest,
The vest,

Make shirt
Dessert. . . .

And though
They go,

I'm told,
For old,

Would rather,
I gather,

Chew
What's new.

But I think I have never more consciously played the rhyme game, in this instance using three-syllable rhymes throughout, than in this:

THE EXTREMELY COMMON COLD

Of all the ills iniquitous,
The cold is most ubiquitous.
It comes to every national,
To sane and to irrational,
To debtor and to creditor,
Illiterate and editor,
To indolent and dutiful,
To ugly and to beautiful,
To modest and to haughty folk,
To pious and to naughty folk,
To high as well as low degree,
To college grad and no degree.
And though you sneeze and cough a lot,
It helps, though not an awful lot,
To know that there's no preference
Regarding colds, or deference,
And even royal highnesses
Have trouble with their sinuses.

It will be noticed in the above examples that there is invariably a little surprise at the end. The last line is, or should be, the nut on the cookie. Of course if the poem is very long, the last line will have to have plenty of punch, almost a knockout blow, or the reader will feel cheated. Charles Lamb once wrote a play, a comedy, the humor of which depended on the disclosure, at the end of the last act, of the screamingly funny name of one of the characters. Well, no name is as funny as all that, and Lamb's play was of course a flop.

So you need a climactic twist or lift at the end of a piece of light verse. But the longer the poem is, the funnier it had better be. This is another reason for the brevity of light verse—unless there can be humor all the way, and perhaps a minor climax at the end of each stanza.

This calls to mind a letter I once received from one of the most astute editors I have ever dealt with. When I get a piece of verse past him, I feel it is really good. Sometimes he grades my poems: A, B plus, C, and so on. I remember one part of his letter (well, I have it here before me) in which he says this:

"I will now explain to you what it is that I think I would like to find in any verse we buy, even though I know that you'll be able to cite a dozen examples right away that don't bear out what I am going to say. What I'd like to see in a verse is a little point in each quatrain that can stand by itself as humor, with the final quatrain bringing the others all together and having the big point in it. I find that too many of the verses sent in to us have nothing but straight exposition in the preliminary stanzas, and the only real point is in the final two, three, or four lines. In other words, most of the verses I send back to the writers have too much water in them. What I really want is a short-short in verse."

You might be interested in a poem of mine that apparently was squeezed dry of water and had something of the quality of a short-short in verse, because this editor not only bought it but gave it one of his rare A grades:

The Love Life (and Death) of a Moose

Up in Newfoundland some 30 moose, mistaking Diesel train horns for mating calls, have been lured to death on the tracks.—*News item.*

Imagine this beast of the frozen Northeast
With its annual amorous craze on,
Seduced by the toot of a choo-choo en route
Into making a fatal liaison.

Conceive of its sighs as it straddles the ties,
Unaware of the killer it's dating.
The honk of the train has gone straight to its brain,
And its mind is completely on mating.

Appalling? Of course, but just think how much worse
It would be, and no words shall we weasel,
Should an engine tear loose from its tracks when a moose
Makes what sounds like the call of a Diesel.

Actually this is not exactly as it appeared in the magazine, but as it was further polished when I included it in *Nights With Armour.* The standards of magazine editors are high, but the standards of book publishers are even higher, and I often have to improve titles and sharpen lines in the verses I choose (with editorial advice) for a collection. After all, the book is likely to be around a good while longer than the issue of the magazine in which the poem first appeared.

The material for light verse comes from many places: newspapers (as in the poem about the moose), casual remarks, odd phrases, and all the assortment of human foibles. An irritation often starts me going on a poem, the way a grain of sand generates a pearl in an oyster, though I do not mean that I always, or ever, produce a pearl. The home, the office, the golf course, the highway, the department store—all of these are full of the raw stuff of humor in verse. The light verse writer must watch the human scene with the eye of a reporter, must read the works of his contemporaries and competitors, must write and re-write and polish. Then he must leave no trace of labor, but make it all look natural and easy.

Light verse may be a minor art but it demands a major effort. You will know when you have written a piece just right, even before an editor tells you. You get that sweet feeling the batter gets when he connects solidly with the ball. You know, without looking, that this one is going over the fence.

JOHN BAILEY *has been associated with humor writing in the capacity of both editor and contributor. A former humor editor of* The Saturday Evening Post *for seven years, Mr. Bailey has since devoted himself to writing. He has sold some 1,000 humorous articles, which have appeared in* The Saturday Evening Post, Esquire, The Reader's Digest, *and many others. His work is also represented in many anthologies and college textbooks on writing. Mr. Bailey is the author of several books. His most recent, written with J. C. Furnas, is* Mr. Webster's Bloomers, or English Bashed and Unabashed (*Morrow*).

IX

HOW SHALL I WORD IT?

BY JOHN BAILEY

A person reading about a familiar thing is halfway towards laughter. This is especially true of writing about familiar things that the reader has not seen mentioned in print before.

Take, for example, a man sneaking a look at himself in a store window. Or a man who drops the top of a toothpaste tube into the wash-basin and scrambles to get it before it goes down the drain. These "shared experience" things are pure gold for the humor writer.

However, a curious phenomenon takes place in writing about these things. As they come to mind, the mind tends

97

to reject them precisely because they have never been written about. Furthermore, they are instinctively rejected at the exact moment they reach the conscious mind.

But the very fact that they have not been mentioned in print is the reason to seize them before they are lost.

Now, although the observation and apprehension of this sort of shared experience may be one of your strengths, perhaps you write too directly about it. Use indirection. Don't tell the reader about it plainly. Let him "get" it. This gives him pleasure and he will sometimes laugh just at "getting" it.

Use dialogue wherever possible, and wherever you have not used some other device to make reading easy or amusing. Ideally, there will be something amusing in every paragraph. This is vital in the opening paragraph. It need not be a genuine gag. The amusing something can be a word or some unexpected phrasing.

After completing an "Hysterical History" piece on the subject of Kansas, I was uneasy about the opening paragraph. Though it was exactly what I wanted to set the stage, it was rather long and it wasn't funny. So I wrote an entirely new paragraph which I tacked on the top:

> Kansas is not perfectly flat as some people suppose. There is a drop of seven feet from the western edge to the eastern edge. A marble, placed on the western edge, would roll all the way across to Missouri.

And a Wilbur piece on thunderstorms begins:

> "Yipe."
> The speaker was my twelve-year-old nephew, Wilbur . . .

Not funny, but attention-getting; and the point is, I devoted a long time to arriving at as good a beginning as possible.

The first few sentences and the last few sentences are by far the most important parts of a short piece. It is important to amuse the reader in the first paragraph, and it is vital to amuse him in the last. If the reader is amused by the first paragraph, he will read on (a surprising distance, sometimes) looking for more. (So will the editor.)

A good (funny) ending will leave a good taste in the mouth. Any piece that leaves a good taste in the mouth is likely to strike the editor as something worth buying. Hence, the overwhelming importance of a good ending.

Writing an ending which refers to the title is a good trick and well worth doing if the piece lends itself to it. Otherwise titles should be amusing in themselves (in which case they can be any length) or they should be inoffensive (in which case they should be as short as possible). The most useful non-funny title is one which either instantly sets the mood ("Squawk!" for a parakeet piece) or one which conveys necessary information quickly (such as "Wilbur Views Television"). And incidentally, a really good title can go a long way towards selling a piece.

When writing a humorous piece, do not write with *The Saturday Evening Post* in mind. Have in mind as your audience one person—your neighbor. Or perhaps a group of two or three persons. If you can make them laugh you will also make the six million *Post* readers laugh—or enough of them to make *The Saturday Evening Post* want to print your piece.

But to say to yourself, in effect, "I will now write a piece for *The Saturday Evening Post,*" can have a stultifying effect. Subconsciously you are out to give them their money's worth.

Once you have chosen a subject to write about (and it's a practical idea to choose something as near the top of people's minds as possible, although not necessarily "around home" or "newsy"), the actual methods of making humor within that subject are various, but some of them can be put down, and these methods can and should be practiced so that they spring to mind as they fit.

One of the most important methods is the *Opposite*. An entire piece can be based on an *Opposite*, and many are. A series of short biographical sketches for the *Post*, with the overall title, "Great Stories of Famous Men," consisted of:

1) A great financier—who never made any money.

2) A great artist—who never painted anything.

3) A great composer—who never wrote any music.

Within a piece, deliberately attempt to contrive opposites (as well as in the other structures which follow). Play with a sentence to see whether half of it can be twisted to form an opposite. ("Plainly the tide is coming in. Or else it is going out.")

In the financier piece the boy is determined to become a great financier. He has great curiosity about the financial world. And he says: "Papa, what is a Corona Corona?" This device may be identified as *A Common Idea Carried to an Extreme* (though it also contains elements of *Displacement* —choosing the less important of two things—and an *Opposite*.)

Any common (shared) idea may be carried to an extreme, but it must be a logical extreme.

When a reader is made to feel superior to a character, it makes him feel good, and feeling good is next door to laughter. One may achieve this with mistakes in grammar (Wilbur) and generally with stupid conduct. This is the reason many pieces written in the first person depict the husband as the goat; these cause women to laugh—and also husbands who feel superior to the poor fish depicted.

But the *Superior* structure should not be confused with the *Sympathetic* structure at which the reader laughs, but not because he feels any superiority to the character. The character is inferior all right, not to the reader but to the general buffeting that life is giving him. So is the reader and he laughs in sympathy. (Man at the income-tax bureau: "I would like to speak to somebody soft-hearted.")

Authority Punctured: A character who represents authority (school teachers and policemen are notorious examples) has that authority ridiculed, lessened, or overcome. Success will depend upon the logic of the situation, the ingeniousness of the device used to puncture authority, and upon the extent to which your audience resents the particular kind of authority involved.

Besides using these humor elements, make permanent written notes of certain devices and basic structures, taken from wherever you see them, and you can refer to these and use them as the opportunity presents itself.

Here is an example from a short story I wrote for *Collier's:*

"And that," concluded the captain, "is the story of the mouse you just saw go in that doorway—one of Jennie's babies, now grown to sturdy, useful mousehood. In gratitude for having brought the two young lovers together (for Bill and Molly are now married) they were given the run of the house."

"Bill and Molly?"

"No. The mice. As you are an animal lover yourself, you will enjoy meeting them."

"The mice?"

"No. Bill and Molly. Though, of course, you will meet *them,* too. When you do, notice how glossy their hair is. It's really surprising how clean they keep themselves."

"Bill and Molly?"
"No. The mice."

This is an example of *Displacement,* or emphasis on the least important element. This device can become familiar to you and can be used constantly. Here is one more example:

Panhandler: "Mister, will you give me a penny? I haven't eaten for six days and I want to weigh myself."

Having chosen a subject to write about, decide on the form. What characters can best be used to express your ideas? A husband and wife? A professor? A workman? What kind of workman?

When writing a piece in the first person assign yourself a characteristic (conceit, arrogance, bumbling, etc.) and stick to it throughout the piece.

Does the idea lend itself to any of the short forms of writing familiar in daily life? (Letters, newspaper columns, circulars, almanacs, scientific reports, speeches, radio programs, quiz forms, etc.) When the form you will use is clear in your mind, begin thinking it over. But do not begin to write yet.

About half my pieces are begun in the form of short notes, and it is a method that I recommend wholeheartedly.

Having once conceived the general body of the piece, and keeping in mind the general form it will take, I think of a single paragraph or piece of dialogue before I do any writing.

In writing the "Famous Composer" piece, I first decided that I would follow the usual short biographical form. I then decided on an all-over opposite; and in this case the opposite was: a great composer who never wrote any music.

I did not begin at the beginning. My immediate problem

was to find something funny that would come early in the piece and which at the same time would set the feel of stupidity for the whole piece—a problem which I felt was solved when the dumb musical prodigy (aged six) saw a violin for the first time and said:

"What's dat, Mama?"

To sum up, choose the subject and decide on the form it will take. When the form is clear in your mind, begin making notes. The main thing at this point is to think of usable snatches of humorous phrasing, without considering continuity as yet. Since you have not yet written anything, these snatches are not guided (and ruined) by what went before. Nothing went before. There is complete free play.

These snatches are milestones and should guide the whole piece. When you have two sheets of random notes, begin to write the piece from the top. Begin by trying for a funny first line or paragraph. Check your notes to see whether you have written (without being aware of it) a line that could start the piece.

Try several starts until you are satisfied that you have an amusing first paragraph. If it won't come, start the piece anyhow and come back to the first paragraph.

Write continuously, putting in everything you need to make the point of the piece, and at the same time lead properly to the humorous high-spots. Leave blanks for such details as dates and persons' names which can be filled in later.

Leave the title until last unless a perfect title springs into your head. If a title does not come easily, write down as many titles as occur to you. Try combining parts of two or more, or transpose some well-known phrase.

When the piece is finished, read each paragraph separately, to see whether any is misplaced. Mentally transpose paragraphs. If your funniest paragraph is in the middle see if you can move it nearer the top.

When you find a dead paragraph (unfunny), see if it can be cut out completely. If not, see if it can be reduced to one sentence. If neither can be done, work over it and change it until it has in it, at the very least, something titillating. However, do not work over a good paragraph. Don't touch it!

When you have written the piece, and polished it, send it to market. Try not to worry about it.

You are now ready to begin a new piece!

X

PREPARING AND SELLING YOUR MANUSCRIPT

By A. S. Burack

Although writing fillers and short humor does not require specialized knowledge or experience, there are some basic techniques for preparing and marketing manuscripts which you will find helpful. The *content* of the material is the editor's chief concern when deciding whether or not to buy a manuscript, but good *form* and neat appearance are always plus factors in editorial eyes. You can also increase your sales by learning as much as possible about markets, by being resourceful in collecting material and by being business-like in submitting manuscripts.

KNOWING THE MARKETS

Every good salesman must know what his customers want to buy. If you hope to sell short items regularly, you should be aware of what the editors are currently purchasing. New writers in the filler and short item field often discover that they are already familiar with many of the existing markets. Your daily or Sunday newspaper, or favorite magazine very likely will welcome your submissions. If you or someone in your family reads a trade paper or business magazine, you'll discover that such specialized publications may also be buying short items.

The quickest and easiest way to find out who will buy fillers, humor, light verse, etc., is to study the available market lists. The market section which follows is a comprehensive listing of publications that will buy such items. Other market lists are printed from time to time in journals for writers.

You should also keep checking the publications themselves, since editorial requirements for fillers and short humor change frequently. A magazine may solicit contributions for a particular column for several months—and then stop purchasing, either because the editor has enough items on hand or because the column is to be replaced by a different feature with different needs. Often, requirements for a column may vary from week to week: if your Sunday newspaper includes the *This Week* supplement, you may have noticed that Bennett Cerf will request limericks or puns one week, jokes about blondes the next, etc., for his popular column, "Cerfboard."

Most of the publications you'll want to study may be found at your local library or newsstand. Libraries subscribe to many different publications, and although current issues generally cannot be taken out, you can keep up with your potential markets by making an occasional visit to the periodical section. Many newsstand dealers understandably object to strangers leafing through dozens of magazines on display, but they are usually willing to let regular customers do some browsing—so patronize one stand as often as you can. Buy something once in a while to retain the dealer's good will. If a magazine is not available at your library or newsstand, you can purchase a sample copy directly from the publisher.

Some writers of short items try to know the needs of many *different* magazines so that they will be able to select a market quickly when they have a suitable idea. Others concentrate on three or four publications they feel they can sell to, and study these carefully. Most writers try to find at least one or two new markets each month—for a change of pace, to replace discontinued markets, or simply to expand their sales possibilities.

COLLECTING MATERIAL

One of the first steps a new writer of short items should take is to set up some method of collecting ideas and information. Perhaps you will decide that a notebook will serve your purpose at the beginning, or possibly you may want a more elaborate filing system.

Some writers keep a file of large envelopes or folders. They decide upon several categories that interest them—either something as specialized as "Bright Sayings of Children" and "Recipes," or more general classifications like "Women's Magazines" and "Outdoor Projects." They then tuck into the files all related material: ideas, information, possible markets, etc. Many writers make a practice of carrying small notebooks with them so that they can jot down an idea the moment they think of one. Later they transfer the notebook pages to the proper files.

You may find it helpful to save printed material that may later be useful—tags on garments, manufacturers' information sheets, etc. Government pamphlets contain many useful facts; you may request specific pamphlets from the Superintendent of Documents, Government Printing Office, Washington 25, D. C., and you may also ask to be put on the free mailing list to receive information about government publications.

HOW TO SUBMIT SHORT ITEMS

In general, the procedure for submitting a short item is the same as that for submitting any manuscript: Prepare a neat, legible manuscript (typed manuscripts are always preferred). Your name and address should be typed in the upper left-hand corner of the first page; the number of words in the upper right-hand corner of the first page. It is not necessary to give the exact number of words in a manuscript. Simply count the number of words in the average line and multiply this by the number of lines on the page. Thus, if you have ten words in an average line, and ten lines of typing, your item is about one hundred words long. The title of the manuscript should be centered, and your by-line goes beneath the title. Often the only title you will have is the title of the column to which you are submitting the item—"Life in These United States," "Grin and Share It," etc. The first page of your manuscript will look like this:

```
John J. Jones                        80 words
54 Willow Road
Anytown 27, New York
          A New Way to Store Scrap Lumber
                   by John J. Jones
```

Often, writers of short items will have more than one item to submit at a time. Each item should be typed double-spaced on a separate sheet, with your name and address on each sheet. If the items are on separate sheets, editors are able to pass around several items for consideration by different departments. Also, if an editor wishes to buy just one item out of the group submitted, he doesn't have to hold a page with other material on it.

How many short items should be submitted at one time? Some writers decide this by discovering how many they can send through the mail for a 4¢ stamp. Remember that you must include a return envelope when weighing your material. In general, not more than four to six items should be submitted together. Many editors dislike reading large batches of material from one person and may feel that an over-prolific writer does not spend enough time on each item.

Short items do not have to be submitted on full sheets of paper. You may divide an 8½ x 11 sheet in half, but do not try to crowd an item onto too small a piece of paper. Leave margins of at least one inch on all sides. Minor corrections may be made in ink, but in general, it is always better to re-type a short item than to submit a soiled or much-corrected manuscript. Editors are always grateful for the manuscript that is neat and easy to read.

Along with your manuscript, enclose a self-addressed, stamped envelope large enough to contain your manuscript, and bearing sufficient postage so that the editor can return your manuscript to you if he cannot use it. Address your item to a department, column or specific editor. You don't need to know the name of the editor; his title, "Filler Editor" or "Handyman Editor" will do.

When you are mailing an item for a particular column in a magazine, be sure to check the rules for submission in a recent issue of the magazine. Sometimes a publication has special rules for submitting material: *Popular Science,* for instance, considers ideas for the column, "I'd Like to See Them Make . . ." but asks that ideas be sent on *government postcards only.*

You do not need to send a letter to accompany your manuscript. Editors understand that you are submitting an item for their consideration when it is addressed and sent to them. Nor do you have to indicate that you are enclosing a self-addressed, stamped envelope for the return of your material if they cannot use it—editors know what the envelope is for. *Never* tell the editor that you hope he buys an item because you need money, etc., or indicate that he ought to accept an item because your friends read his magazine and think your item is perfect for it. Such letters stamp you as a rank amateur and editors are not favorably influenced by them.

However, it is a good idea to enclose a covering letter if you have a unique background or training that makes you especially qualified to write on a particular subject. For instance, if you are a professional dietician and submit special recipes, let the editor know about your background and training so that he is aware that you speak with authority on your subject.

Do not send a manuscript to more than one market at a time. If a manuscript is returned by the first market you select, then you may submit it to a second, etc. Many magazines do not return short items at all, and indicate this policy somewhere on their pages along with a statement noting the amount of time that must elapse before an item can be considered rejected. You must observe this waiting period before you submit your item to another market.

Make a carbon copy of any item you submit. (It is especially important to retain carbon copies of items sent to publications that do not return manuscripts.) In cases where magazines require printed clippings, record the pertinent facts about these on a file card. (If a magazine follows a no-return policy, it generally makes no exception, even if you hopefully enclose a self-addressed stamped envelope—so you may forfeit those printed clippings.)

Keep track of the date when you mail a manuscript so that if a publication states, "Items not accepted within six weeks can be considered rejected," you know when your six-week waiting period will expire. For income tax purposes, you'll want to know how much money you've received and who paid you. If a holiday or seasonal item doesn't sell one year, you may want to know where you submitted it and what the editor's comments were. Sometimes an editor will indicate that he is currently overstocked, and request that you re-submit at a later date.

Perhaps the simplest method of keeping a record is to use the back of your carbon copy of the manuscript. Note the name and address of the magazine and the date the item was submitted. If the item is accepted, note this and the amount received. If the item is rejected, note this, plus any pertinent editorial comment. Clip any related papers—letters, sales contracts, etc.—to the carbon copy. When an item is accepted, you will probably want to transfer the carbon from a "Submitted" file to an "Accepted" file, so plan to keep at least two files.

Another method often used by writers calls for two files of 3 x 5 cards. The cards in one file contain the history of each item submitted (the title, number of words, where and when submitted, etc.). When an item is accepted, the appropriate information is noted on its card, which is then transferred to the other file.

Most editors try to accept or reject manuscripts as promptly as possible, but often you will have to wait as long as six weeks for a report. Occasionally even more time will go by without any word from an editor. If you are sure that a magazine makes it a policy to return manuscripts, and you haven't received any report in two months, write a polite note to the editor, asking if he received your submission. Enclose a self-addressed stamped envelope for his reply. Sometimes manuscripts do get lost in the mail and often reports are delayed because of staff absences or changes in editors; if you do inquire about a manuscript, most editors will try to let you know promptly what has happened.

Sometimes, when a magazine accepts your item, you will receive a contract or release that you must sign and return. The contract usually asks you to certify that the item is original, and states the terms of the sale (in most cases, the magazine buys all rights). You are safe in accepting the terms of a contract from any reputable publisher.

IT IS TIME TO BEGIN

You alone can supply the essential qualities that will insure your success in writing and selling fillers and short humor. You must be willing to keep writing and sending out your manuscripts. Don't allow yourself to become discouraged—many an item has been sold on its fifteenth or even twentieth trip to market. Look and listen for ideas, write them up, pick appropriate markets, and then submit your manuscripts. Only then can you feel the sense of accomplishment and anticipation that all writers share. Your manuscript may come back with a rejection slip— send it to the next market on your list! But you may also receive a check—not only a reward in itself, but a promise that your name and writing will appear in print. From that moment on, you are a selling writer.

PART II

WHERE TO SELL

NOTE

The following list of markets for fillers and short humor was compiled from questionnaires that were sent to the editors of more than 1,500 publications. The editors were asked to list what types of short items they buy, length requirements, and rate and time of payment. Only publications which *pay* for short items have been listed.

Although extreme care has been taken to have the information accurate, the needs of editors vary from time to time, and there will undoubtedly be some changes in the requirements as listed. Some new magazines may come into existence, and others now being published may be suspended. A few well-known magazines are currently not purchasing short items, and they asked not to be listed at this time, but their needs may change. It is usually advisable for writers to check recent issues of publications before submitting manuscripts.

MANUSCRIPT MARKETS

ACTION—American Baptist Board of Education and Publication, Valley Forge, Pa. 19481.
Monthly religious magazine for youth. Uses some short humorous filler material. Pays 1¢ a word, on acceptance.

ADVENTURE—Harvest Publications, 5750 North Ashland Ave., Chicago, Ill. 60626.
Evangelical Christian publication for children, 9 to 12. Novelty features with a definite religious (evangelical) point, 100 to 500 words. Pays 2½¢ a word and up, on acceptance. Information packet and samples for this and other papers available for 50¢.

ARGOSY—Fleetway Publications, Ltd., 300 East 42nd St., 15th Floor, New York, N.Y. 10017.
English general interest magazine. Uses light humorous verse, fillers, humor, puzzles, to 200 words. Pays on acceptance.

ALASKA SPORTSMAN—Box 1271, Juneau, Alaska 99801.
Monthly devoted to life in Alaska. Uses short articles, from 100 words, with pictures, on subjects covering "life on the last frontier." Also uses good cartoons (Alaska-Yukon subject matter only). Pays $10 to $25 for short prose.

THE ALLIED YOUTH—1901 Fort Myer Dr., Arlington, Va.
Short stories, under 1,200 words. Pays 2¢ a word, on publication.

THE AMERICAN FIELD—222 West Adams St., Chicago, Ill. 60606.
Short fact items and anecdotes on outdoor sports, recreational activities, and field trials for bird dogs. Payment varies and is on acceptance.

AMERICAN FRUIT GROWER—Willoughby, Ohio 44094.
For commercial fruit growers. Short fact items, 100 to 200 words, pertaining to fruit production and marketing. Pays about 1¢ a word, on acceptance.

THE AMERICAN HOME—641 Lexington Ave., New York, N. Y. 10022.
Wants short, pre-front articles dealing with the home and its environment. No fiction. Prefers solid, service-type articles giving factual information. Pays on acceptance.

AMERICAN LEGION MAGAZINE—720 Fifth Ave., New York, N. Y. 10019.
Wants original anecdotes (up to 300 words), epigrams, humorous and light verse (up to 16 lines). Pays $2.50 per line of verse, $10 per epigram, and $20 per anecdote. Address manuscripts to "Parting Shots" Editor.

THE AMERICAN RIFLEMAN—1600 Rhode Island Ave., N.W., Washington, D.C. 20036.
Uses material on all types of small arms. Short features, 500 to 750 words. Pays on acceptance.

THE AMERICAN SOFT DRINK JOURNAL—777 West Peachtree St., N.E., Atlanta, Ga. 30308.
Illustrated shorts, 200 to 500 words, on advertising, merchandising, and selling of carbonated beverages. Pays 1¢ a word and up.

AMERICAN VEGETABLE GROWER—Willoughby, Ohio 44094.
For commercial vegetable growers. Short fact items, 100 to 200 words, pertaining to vegetable production and marketing. Pays about 1¢ a word, on acceptance.

THE AOPA PILOT—4644 East-West Highway, Bethesda, Md. 20014.
For private and business aviation. Short items, 100 to 300 words, one photo, about a personality or a new development of interest. Pays 5¢ a word and $5 to $10 for photos, on acceptance.

THE AQUARIUM—Curren Arcade Bldg., 53 East Main St., Norristown, Pa. 19404.
Short items, 250 words and up, on tropical fish, fish breeding, and fish collecting, with photos. Pays 1¢ a word, $1.50 to $5 for photos. Query first.

ARIZONA WILDLIFE SPORTSMAN—3300 North Central, Phoenix, Ariz. 85012.
Short fact items on outdoor subjects. Also features and fiction about outdoor Arizona and the Southwest. Payment on publication.

THE ATLANTIC—8 Arlington St., Boston, Mass. 02116.
Short humor and light writing, 500 to 1,500 words, for the monthly department, "Accent on Living." Payment is up to $200, on acceptance.

BABY TALK—149 Madison Ave., New York, N. Y.
True experience pieces, from 500 words, by mother or father, on baby, baby care, family relations, etc. "Your Opinion" department uses short articles expressing a point of view rather than experience.

BALLROOM DANCE MAGAZINE—268 West 47th St., New York, N. Y. 10036.
Occasional fillers related to ballroom dancing. Pays on publication.

BASEBALL DIGEST—1708 Second St., Highland Park, Ill. 60035.
Fillers and humor on professional baseball topics. Pays by arrangement.

BEST FOR MEN—See *The Men's Digest.*

BETTER HOMES & GARDENS—1716 Locust St., Des Moines, Iowa 50303.
Not in the market for fillers at this time. Authors should watch magazine for announcements of special columns which buy short items.

BITS AND PIECES—Box 746, Newcastle, Wyoming 82701.
Short fillers on the history of Wyoming and the surrounding states.
Source of information must be given. Length: 500 to 1,000 words.
Pays 1¢ a word, on publication.

BLACK BELT—5650 West Washington Blvd., Los Angeles, Calif. 90016.
Articles, from 200 words, on judo, ju-jitsu, karate, aikido, kendo, and
other Oriental arts and sports of self-defense. Pays various rates.

BOOT & SHOE RECORDER—56th and Chestnut Sts., Philadelphia, Pa.
19139.
Short-short picture-caption stories, 100 to 300 words, that detail merchandising ideas at the retail level. Also feature stories, from 300
words, about successful merchandising ideas of shoe stores and departments, retail problems, new production techniques, industry
trends. Must be specific. Also trade news. Pays $30 and up per page
for features, $3 and up for trade news. Query first.

BOSTON MAGAZINE—125 High St., Boston, Mass. 02110.
Short filler material of local interest. For "Arrivals & Departures"
column, uses items 150 to 350 words. Pays $15 to $35.

BREEZY—See *Humorama, Inc.*

BROADSIDE—7311 Fulton Ave., North Hollywood, Calif. 91605.
Men's magazine. Uses short humor, to 1,800 words. Pays $75 to $100.

BUSINESS MANAGEMENT—22 West Putnam Ave., Greenwich, Conn.
06830.
For top management in large companies. Uses 50- to 150-word "Workshop for Management" items. Pays $10 per item. See magazine before
submitting.

CALLING ALL GIRLS—See *Young Miss.*

CAMPING GUIDE—215 Park Ave. South, New York, N. Y. 10003.
Magazine dealing with practical aspects of family camping. Uses one
or two cartoons per issue. Pays $10, on publication.

CAMPS AND CONFERENCES—Gundersen Dr. and Schmale Rd.,
Wheaton, Ill. 60187.
Publication of the Christian Camps and Conferences Association. For
camp directors and managers. Uses fillers and short (600 to 800
words) articles either inspirational or on specific aspects of camp life.
Pays on publication.

CAMPUS LIFE—North Main St., Wheaton, Ill.
Magazine for Christian youth (13 to 19). Teen-slanted cartoons and
jokes. Pays $5 per cartoon; $1 per short joke.

CANADIAN HOMES MAGAZINE—60 Yonge St., Toronto 1, Ontario,
Canada.
Newspaper supplement. Short, well-illustrated pieces on practical
ideas for home decorating and renovating, or on outdoor living. All

pieces should have a strong how-to emphasis and projects must be suitable to Canadian conditions. Query first. Payment is from $10 to $100. Address Short Features Editor.

CAR AND DRIVER—One Park Ave., New York, N. Y. 10016.
Automotive magazine. Uses occasional fillers. Pays $10 to $25.

CATHOLIC DIGEST—44 East 53rd St., New York, N. Y. 10022.
For "Hearts are Trumps" feature, wants original accounts, under 300 words, of true cases where unseeking kindness was rewarded. For "The Open Door," true incidents by which persons were brought into the Church. For "The Perfect Assist," original reports of tactful remarks or actions. $50 for each item. Also needed is material for "People Are Like That," illustrating instinctive goodness of human nature, and amusing or inspiring tales for "In Our Parish" and "In Our House." Pays $20 for each item. Pays $4 for acceptable "Flights of Fancy," picturesque figures of speech, with exact source given. All payments on publication. Fillers not acknowledged or returned.

CATS—4 Smithfield St., Pittsburgh, Pa. 15222.
Poems, preferably light, about cats, up to 20 lines. Pays 20¢ a line, on acceptance.

CHANGING TIMES: *The Kiplinger Magazine*—1729 H St., N.W., Washington, D. C. 20006.
Epigrams and topical quips, one or two sentences, for "Notes on These Changing Times" page. Payment is $5 per item.

CHATELAINE—481 University Ave., Toronto 2, Ont., Canada.
Light verse. Pays $10 to $15.

CHICAGO TRIBUNE—Tribune Tower, Chicago, Ill. 60611.
Uses short items, up to 200 words, about personal experiences in "What Kids Say," "I'll Never Forget," and "I'll Never Live It Down" columns in Sunday Features section. Payment is $5, on publication.

CHILD LIFE—1100 Waterway Blvd., Indianapolis, Ind. 46207.
Monthly for children. Uses fillers and short humor, poetry of any length. Pays about 3¢ a word for prose, from 25¢ a line for verse.

THE CHRISTIAN ADVENTURER—Messenger Publishing House, P.O. Box 850, Joplin, Mo. 64802.
Weekly Sunday school paper for teen-agers. Uses inspirational fillers. Pays ¼¢ a word, on publication.

THE CHRISTIAN BOOKSELLER—Gundersen Dr. and Schmale Rd., Wheaton, Ill. 60187.
Business magazine for religious bookstore dealers and owners. Brief (250 words) examples of the "Extra Dividend" in bookselling, where books or supplies sold produce unusual or long-range results. Also uses cartoons. Pays $10 for "Extra Dividend" column, $5 per cartoon, on publication.

THE CHRISTIAN HOME—201 Eighth Ave. South, Nashville, Tenn. 37203.
Methodist. Humorous, seasonal or inspirational verse, to 16 lines, of interest to parents. Pays 50¢ a line, on acceptance.

THE CHRISTIAN MOTHER—8121 Hamilton Ave., Cincinnati, Ohio 45231.
A guide for Christian child training. Uses material for fathers' page, and pages with creative children's activities. "How We Did It" page uses brief suggestions from mothers about their methods of building Christian homes. Pays various rates, on publication.

THE CHRISTIAN SCIENCE MONITOR—One Norway St., Boston, Mass. 02115. Address material to Herbert E. Thorson, Editor, Family Features Page.
Uses fillers and shorts (not fact fillers); anecdotes; puzzles of the quiz variety; light verse of various lengths; true accounts of outstanding courage, kindness, good-neighbor policy, for "Sundial" feature. Also has "As the Small Fry See It," a column of children's sayings. Payment twice a month, covering material accepted or used in the preceding two-week interim. Photos, $5 to $10; "Small Fry," $2; "Sundials," $3; varies for light verse.

THE CHURCH MUSICIAN—127 Ninth Ave. North, Nashville, Tenn. 37203.
Southern Baptist. Fillers, puzzles, cartoons with a musical touch. Pays about 2¢ a word, on acceptance.

COLUMBIA — Box 1670, New Haven, Conn. 06507.
Official journal of the Knights of Columbus. Directed to a general Catholic audience. Uses short humor or satire features, to 1,000 words, fillers of about 100 words, and cartoons, "showing pungent, wordless humor." Pays up to $100 for short humor, $10 for fillers, and $25 for cartoons, on acceptance.

COMEDY MAGAZINE—See *Humorama, Inc.*

COMPETITION PRESS & AUTOWEEK—Autoweek Bldg., Lafayette, Calif. 94549.
Weekly newspaper covering news of all motor sports. Uses automotive news items and features to 1,200 words, and cartoons. Pays $1 per column inch for prose, $10 for cartoons.

DAVID C. COOK PUBLISHING CO.—850 North Grove Ave., Elgin, Ill.
Protestant evangelical material for teens in Sunday schools. Jokes, puns, puzzles, true-life anecdotes, relating to "lesson theme" of the week. (List available on request.) Pays 2¢ to 4¢ a word. Query first for specific needs.

COSMOPOLITAN—1775 Broadway, New York, N. Y. 10019.
Not in the market for fillers. Authors should watch magazine for announcements of special columns which buy short items.

THE COUNTRY GUIDE—1760 Ellice Ave., Winnipeg 21, Manitoba, Canada.
Puzzles, light verse, hints, and items on home and family subjects—home management, handicrafts, health, child care, etc. Pays 3¢ a word and up, on acceptance.

CUE—20 West 43rd St., New York, N. Y. 10036.
Short features, 1,300 words, about New York City or suburbs, with entertainment angle. Pays from $120, on publication.

CURTAIN AND DRAPERY DEPARTMENT MAGAZINE—230 Fifth Ave., New York, N. Y. 10001.
Uses 250-word merchandising tips. Pays 3¢ a word, on publication.

CYCLE WORLD—745 West Third St., Long Beach, Calif. 90812.
Humor of interest to motorcycle enthusiasts. Material must be accurate and reflect favorably on the sport. Pays 5¢ a word, on publication.

DAILY MEDITATION—Box 2710, San Antonio, Texas 78206.
Nonsectarian religious magazine. Fillers to 350 words. Pays ½¢ to 1¢ a word, on acceptance.

DARE—1626 Magnolia Ct., Cleveland, Ohio 44106.
Men's magazine. "Light, satirical, tongue-in-cheek, iconoclastic, with the purpose of urging men to live up to their potential." Uses short, offbeat filler items, and short articles, 300 to 650 words, with an impact. For "Mind Your Own Business," "Classified" and "Breakout" columns, uses items 100 to 125 words. Pays various rates, on acceptance.

DATEBOOK—71 Washington Place, New York, N. Y. 10011.
Monthy for teen-agers. Uses about ten regular reader-contributed contests, dealing with dating problems, teen fads, room decoration, etiquette, money-making ideas, etc. Payment is from $1 to $10.

THE DELTA REVIEW—4646 Poplar Ave., Memphis, Tenn.
Regional magazine. Especially interested in Southern writers. Uses some humor. Pays various rates, on publication.

DIXIE-ROTO—*The Times-Picayune,* Lafayette Sq., New Orleans, La. 70140.
Original jokes; historical anecdotes related to Louisiana. Pays $2 to $3 for jokes, $10 for anecdotes, on publication.

DODGE NEWS MAGAZINE—5435 West Fort St., Detroit, Mich.
Travel and general interest magazine for Dodge owners. Interested in suggestions only for filler or short humor series.

DOORWAY—Cooperative Book Centre of Canada, Ltd., 66 Northline Rd., Toronto 16, Canada.
Small promotional house organ can use cartoons, jokes, humorous

fillers and short verse suitable for its audience of teacher-librarians and librarians. Pays $10 for cartoons, and from $2 to $5 for short fillers, in Canadian funds, on acceptance.

DOWN EAST—Camden, Maine.
True anecdotes and stories about Maine, up to 800 words, for "It Happened Down East." Pays $5, on acceptance.

EBONY—1820 South Michigan Ave., Chicago, Ill. 60616.
"Speaking of People" column accepts items, up to 200 words, on Negroes in jobs heretofore close to Negroes. Material must describe job, how obtained, training, etc. Human interest angle helpful. Payment is $10 and up, on publication.

ELKS MAGAZINE—425 West Diversey Parkway, Chicago, Ill. 60614.
Short, humorous material of interest to Elks membership. Very sophisticated or lowbrow material should be avoided. Payment starts at 10¢ a word, on acceptance. Query first.

THE EMPIRE MAGAZINE—*Denver Post,* Denver, Colo. 80202.
Weekly rotogravure supplement. Photo-illustrated shorts or fillers on subjects of interest to Rocky Mountain readers. Pays 3¢ a word, plus $5 for each photo.

ESQUIRE—488 Madison Ave., New York, N. Y. 10022.
Short humor, short fact items, and extended letters (for "Aftermath") on articles in the magazine. Payment on acceptance.

ESQUIRE'S GOOD GROOMING MAGAZINE—488 Madison Ave., New York, N. Y. 10022.
Semi-annual publication on good grooming for men. Uses humor from 750 words and fillers, dealing with aspects of good grooming: fashion, etiquette, "how-to," accessories, etc. Pays on acceptance.

EVERYBODY'S POULTRY MAGAZINE—Hanover, Pa. 17331.
Shorts, 100 to 300 words, on commercial poultry production in the Northeastern states. Cartoons. Pays 3¢ a word and up, $5 for cartoons, on acceptance.

FAMILY CIRCLE—488 Madison Ave., New York, N. Y. 10022.
Hints of 100 words or less for "Good Cook's Tips" (cooking), "Shortcuts to Better Housekeeping" (household hints), and "How Did You Handle It?" (child care). Pays $2 to $10 per item, on publication. Submissions cannot be returned.

THE FAMILY HANDYMAN—800 Second Ave., New York, N. Y. 10017.
For do-it-yourself home owners. Short pieces, with photos, 100 to 300 words, on better ways to make or fix something for the "Tips You Should Know About" column. Pays $5 to $10, on publication.

FAMILY WEEKLY—405 Park Ave., New York, N. Y.
Light verse; quips and jokes for "Quips and Quotes" column. Pays on acceptance.

FARM JOURNAL—Washington Sq., Philadelphia, Pa. 19105.
Light verse, quips, jokes, housekeeping shortcuts of 30 to 50 words each; short how-to-make handicraft features. "Passed by the Non-Sensor" uses brief verse and jokes. Payment is $2 to $5 per item, on acceptance. Humorous 3- or 4-line quips of country editors for "Country Press."

FATE—Highland House, 500 Hyacinth Pl., Highland Park, Ill. 60035.
Monthly. True stories and articles on the paranormal, the strange and the unexplained. Uses occasional fillers; also purchases short items, 300 to 600 words, for "True Mystic Experiences" and "My Proof of Survival" columns. Pays $1 to $3 for short fillers, $5 for column items, usually before publication. Queries welcomed.

FATE'S ASTROLOGY FORECAST—Highland House, 500 Hyacinth Pl., Highland Park, Ill. 60035.
Quarterly. Uses all types of filler material pertaining to astrology, up to 600 words. "Ask Forecast" column uses questions and answers regarding astrological points. Pays $3 to $25, depending on length, before publication. Queries welcomed.

FORD TIMES—Ford Motor Co., The American Rd., Dearborn, Mich. 48121.
Uses some humor related to car ownership, travel, recreation. Pays 10¢ a word and up. Query first.

FRIENDS—Warner Press, Inc., Publication Board of the Church of God, Anderson, Ind. 46011.
Church school paper for junior age boys and girls. Short articles, 150 to 500 words on Christian biography, nature, music, sports, travel, things to make and do, vocations and books. Also puzzles, ideas for family fun. Pays various rates, within 30 days of acceptance.

FRONTIER TIMES—See *True West.*

FUN HOUSE—See *Humorama, Inc.*

FUTURE MAGAZINE—Boulder Park, Box 7, Tulsa, Okla.
Published by The United States Jaycees. Biographical or self-improvement articles, from 500 words, for young professional men. Pays 3¢ to 5¢ a word, on acceptance.

GEE-WHIZ—See *Humorama, Inc.*

GEORGIA MAGAZINE—Box 4047, Decatur, Ga. 30031.
Regional publication. General interest, with emphasis on history, heritage, folklore, people, scenic beauty, industries and vacation opportunities of Georgia. Uses short poems and humorous verse, 4 to 6 lines, and short items pertaining to Georgia history, legend, personalities, humorous anecdotes, 300 words or less. Pays $2 to $3 for short verse, $3 to $5 for anecdotes or "Georgettes" (little stories with a Georgia flavor), on publication.

GOLF—800 Second Ave., New York, N. Y. 10017.
Short articles, to 500 words, on topics of national interest to golfers. Cartoons. Pays $50 to $150 for short articles, $50 for cartoons. Query first.

GOLF DIGEST MAGAZINE—88 Scribner Ave., Norwalk, Conn. 06856.
Short fact items, anecdotes, quips, jokes, and light verse. For "Links Laughs," wants true humorous or odd incidents, up to 200 words. Pays 10¢ a word minimum, on acceptance; $10 for "Links Laughs."

GOLFDOM—800 Second Ave., New York, N. Y. 10017.
For the golf superintendent, golf pro, and club manager. Uses fillers, short humor, and jokes. Pays various rates.

GOOD HOUSEKEEPING—959 Eighth Ave., New York, N. Y. 10019.
Buys filler material (anecdotes and epigrams), verse and non-verse for the Light Housekeeping page, and humorous pieces (800 to 1,000 words). Also personal narratives for "My Problem and How I Solved It" series. Pays $5 a line and up for verse, $50 and up for humorous items, more for longer material.

GOOD READING—The Sunshine Press, State & Henrichs Sts., Litchfield, Ill.
Uses success tips, not over 100 words. Payment is based on merit, is on acceptance.

GOSPEL CARRIER—Messenger Publishing House, P.O. Box 850, Joplin, Mo. 64802.
Weekly adult Sunday school paper. Uses inspirational filler material. Pays ¼¢ a word, on publication.

GOURMET MAGAZINE—777 Third Ave., New York, N. Y. 10017.
Light verse with a sophisticated food or drink angle. Payment is on acceptance.

GUNS & AMMO—5959 Hollywood Blvd., Los Angeles, Calif. 90028.
Uses some filler material related to guns and ammunition: tips concerning guns and accessories, hunting secrets, new uses for old gear, quick repairs, or related subjects. Prefers subjects that can be kept to a page or less. Pays $50. Reports within two weeks.

HARLE CROSSWORDS—17 West 44th St., New York, N. Y. 10036.
Crossword puzzle magazines. Write for requirements before submitting material. Pays various rates, on publication.

HARPER'S BAZAAR—572 Madison Ave., New York, N. Y. 10022.
A fashion magazine. Serious and sometimes light poetry of the highest quality, 8 to 40 lines. Payment is $1 a line, on acceptance.

HARPER'S MAGAZINE—2 Park Ave., New York, N. Y. 10016.
Short, humorous items with a significant point, dealing with some aspect of American life. Pays on acceptance.

HOME LIFE—127 Ninth Ave. North, Nashville, Tenn. 37203.
Southern Baptist. Addressed to parents. Uses fillers, 100 to 500 words, on anything that points up family relationships. Pays 2¢ a word, on acceptance.

HOOFS AND HORNS—4444 East Broadway, Tucson, Arizona 85711.
Western fact magazine on horses, rodeos, and cattle. Uses 4-, 8-, 12-, and 16-line verse, usually humorous, with a Western slant. Also uses short news items pertaining to subjects covered by magazine. Pays 2¢ a word and up.

HUMAN EVENTS—410 First St., S.W., Washington, D. C. 20003.
Weekly political newspaper. Short jokes, quips, anecdotes, etc., that would appeal to political conservatives. Length: 100 words or less. Pays 10¢ a word, on publication. Does not acknowledge contributions, except when accepted for publication.

HUMORAMA, INC.—136 East 57th St., New York, N. Y. 10022.
Topical satire, epigrams, humorous fillers, up to 1,000 words. Light verse, up to 48 lines. Pays 75¢ for one-line fillers, 40¢ a line for verse and 3½¢ a word for prose, just before publication. Same address and requirements for *Comedy Magazine, Fun House, Gee-Whiz, Jest, Joker, Laugh Digest, Laugh Riot, Romp,* and *Zip!*

JACK AND JILL—Curtis Publishing Co., Independence Sq., Philadelphia, Pa. 19105.
For children 4 to 12. Short, humorous poems, puzzles, word games. Payment varies.

JEM—550 Fifth Ave., New York, N. Y. 10036.
Men's magazine. "Putting Women in Their Place" uses short, appropriate fillers. Payment is $5 per item, on acceptance.

JEST—See *Humorama, Inc.*

THE JEWELERS' CIRCULAR-KEYSTONE—56th and Chestnut Sts., Philadelphia, Pa. 19139.
Uses 200- to 300-word shorts, focusing sharply on some single activity that built traffic and sales or cut costs for a jeweler or jewelry department in a department store. Pays $10, on acceptance.

JOKER—See *Humorama, Inc.*

JUNIOR HI CHALLENGE—Church of God, 922 Montgomery Ave., Cleveland, Tenn. 37311.
Sunday School lesson and take-home paper. Uses verse, fillers, puzzles, and cartoons. Also prayers and Scriptures for memorization for "Devotions" column. Length: 500 to 600 words. Pays ½¢ a word for short items, $1 for poems, $3 for cartoons, on acceptance.

JUNIOR MESSENGER—General Conference Mennonite Church Board of Education and Publication, 722 Main St., Box 347, Newton, Kansas.

Sunday School story paper for junior-age children. Uses puzzles, short fact items, and light verse. Length for short items, 100 words. Pays ½¢ a word for prose, 10¢ a line for poetry.

THE JUNIOR MUSICIAN—127 Ninth Ave. North, Nashville, Tenn. 37203.
Publishes music puzzles, games, quizzes, cartoons, miscellaneous filler items and illustrated material on making simple instruments, sound experiments.

KANROM, INC.—311 West 43rd St., New York, N. Y. 10036.
Humorous jokes, cartoons, suitable for adult humor calendar. Pays $5 per joke, $10 per cartoon.

LADIES' HOME JOURNAL—641 Lexington Ave., New York, N. Y. 10022.
Not in the market for filler material. Authors should watch magazine for announcements of special columns which buy short items.

LADY'S CIRCLE—777 Third Ave., New York, N. Y. 10017.
Women's magazine. Short verse, fillers, and humor of interest to homemakers. Pays on acceptance.

LAUGH DIGEST—See *Humorama, Inc.*

LAUGH RIOT—See *Humorama, Inc.*

LEATHERNECK—Box 1918, Washington, D. C. 20013.
Magazine for the enlisted Marine. Short fact items about Marine personalities or activities. Pays $10 to $15. Light, Marine-slanted verse. Pays $10 and up, depending on length. All payment on acceptance.

THE LION—209 North Michigan Ave., Chicago, Ill. 60601.
Magazine for international readership of business and professional men. Cartoons and short humor. Pays various rates. Query first.

LIQUOR STORE—820 Second Ave., New York, N. Y. 10017.
Trade monthly on wine and liquor store merchandising. Short items to 500 words, with action photos. Cartoons. Pays 3¢ a word and up.

LOOK—488 Madison Ave., New York, N. Y. 10022.
Typos and amusing editorial lapses from newspapers and other printed sources. Pays $10. Also uses some short humorous verse. Queries on humor items should be directed to Mr. J. M. Flagler, Humor Editor.

THE LOS ANGELES MAGAZINE—271 North Canon Dr., Beverly Hills, Calif.
Humor and satire directed to a sophisticated Southern California readership. Contributors should be familiar with the area and current interests of its inhabitants. Pays 4¢ a word, on publication.

MACLEAN'S MAGAZINE—481 University Ave., Toronto 2, Ont., Canada.
General Canadian magazine. Filler material: for "Parade" feature,

brief topical anecdotes drawn from the Canadian scene; pays $5 to $10; for "Canadianecdotes," 200 to 500 words on some event in Canada's past. Source material is essential. Pays $75.

McCALL'S—230 Park Ave., New York, N. Y. 10017.
Women's magazine. Humorous and light verses are considered. Payment is $5 a line, on acceptance.

MALE—625 Madison Ave., New York, N. Y. 10022.
Uses jokes of interest to men. Submissions must be typewritten or legible, and cannot be returned. No poetry. Pays $5 per joke, on acceptance. Same address and requirements for *Men, Man's World,* and *True Action.*

MAN'S WORLD—See *Male.*

MARRIAGE: *The Magazine of Catholic Family Living*—St. Meinrad, Indiana.
For "We Tried This," wants short, personal accounts up to 400 words, telling about original solutions to family problems. For "At Our House," wants short, personal accounts of unusual or amusing incidents of family living, up to 400 words. Pays $15, on acceptance. Also uses short articles, 400 to 800 words, giving personal accounts of memorable experiences in marriage: "How We Met," "Our Most Remembered Experience in Marriage," "The Best Advice We Ever Received," etc. Payment for these is $20, on acceptance.

MATURE YEARS—Methodist Publishing House, 201 Eighth Ave. South, Nashville, Tenn. 37202.
For older adults. Uses occasional short items, to 1,000 words. Pays 2¢ a word, on acceptance.

MECHANIX ILLUSTRATED—67 West 44th St., New York, N. Y. 10036.
Buys single photos with captions, tips illustrated by rough drawings, or un-illustrated tips for short cuts in the shop, garage, or home. Departments include Home Kinks, Home & Shop Shorts, Freddie Fumbles (cartoon strip), Farmer's Page, Inventions Wanted (ideas for inventions from readers), and MIMI (unusual new products shown with girl "product tester"). Also buys cartoons and short one-column and half-column fillers, to 500 words. Rates: captioned photos, $20; tips with drawing, to $15; un-illustrated tips, $5; cartoons, $30; Inventions Wanted ideas, $5; Freddie Fumbles ideas, $10; finder's fee for MIMI products, $50; one-column fillers, $75.

MEDICAL ECONOMICS—Oradell, N. J.
Short, true-to-life anecdotes about doctors. Pays $25 to $75, per anecdote. Write for "Guide to Contributors" and sample copy.

MEN—See *Male.*

THE MEN'S DIGEST—2715 North Pulaski Rd., Chicago, Ill. 60639.
Men's magazine. Humorous verse, 10 to 12 lines, with a strong male

slant. Pays on acceptance. Same address and requirements for *Best for Men* and *Rascal*.

THE MIRACAN MERCHANDISER—American Can Company, 100 Park Ave., New York, N. Y. 10017.
Very short (200 to 300 words) photo stories about canned carbonated beverage producers, retailers, distributors, and canners. Pays $20 and up, on acceptance.

MODERATOR—115 South 37th St., Philadelphia, Pa. 19104.
Magazine for college students, about student affairs and problems. Can use relevant fillers and short humor. Pays 1½¢ a word, on publication.

MODERN BRIDE—One Park Ave., New York, N. Y. 10016.
Short items directed to the bride around the time of her wedding. Payment, from $10 to $75.

MODERN PHOTOGRAPHY—165 West 46th St., New York, N. Y. 10036.
Buys photographic how-to-do-its, 250 to 300 words. Pays $10 to $15 for test and photograph, on acceptance.

MONSIEUR—550 Fifth Ave., New York, N. Y. 10036.
Men's magazine. "Monsieur on the Boulevard" uses amusing anecdotes, preferably with a continental background. Payment is $5 per item, on acceptance.

MOTOR BOATING—959 Eighth Ave., New York, N. Y. 10019.
Buys short fact items, anecdotes and hints on boating subjects. Pays varying rates, on acceptance.

MOTOR TREND—8490 Sunset Blvd., Los Angeles, Calif. 90069.
General interest automotive magazine. Uses humorous fillers, whimsy, reminiscences, practical how-to's, travel tips, etc., all automotive oriented, 400 to 800 words, and 2 to 3 photos, where applicable. Authors should see recent issues for special columns which use short items, such as "Cars a la Carte" and "Spotlight on Detroit." Pays $35 to $150, more for exceptional material, on acceptance.

MOTOR WEST—Box 650, Orange, Calif. 92669.
Success stories, short articles, humor, cartoons, about auto repair shops, service stations, or garages in 13 Western states only. Pays on publication. Query first.

MUSIC JOURNAL—1776 Broadway, New York, N. Y. 10019.
Fillers and short items on some aspect of music. Token payment, by arrangement, on publication.

THE NATIONAL GUARDSMAN—1 Massachusetts Ave., N.W., Washington, D. C. 20001.
Army National Guard and Air National Guard magazines. For "Tales from the Troops," wants military anecdotes, 150 to 250 words. Payment is $10, on publication.

THE NATIONAL OBSERVER—11501 Columbia Pike, Silver Spring, Md.
Short anecdotes, nostalgic items, and full-length features, from 300 to 2,000 words. No fillers. Payment is $10 to $100 per item.

NATIONAL REVIEW—150 East 35th St., New York, N. Y. 10016.
Conservative political journal. Uses short satirical poems, 4 to 30 lines, and short prose satire, up to 200 words. Payment is $10 to $15, on publication.

NATIONAL WILDLIFE—534 North Broadway, Milwaukee, Wisc. 53202.
Uses material related to wildlife, conservation, and recreation, which is or can be illustrated: one-liners, 1-pagers, and longer articles. Cartoons. Pays $25 and up per page, $25 and up for cartoons, on acceptance. Query first.

NEW—Unity School of Christianity, Lee's Summit, Mo. 64063.
Uses fillers up to 600 words stressing the art of living, and inspirational poems. Pays 2¢ a word and up for fillers, 25¢ a line and up for poems, on acceptance.

THE NEW YORK TIMES MAGAZINE—229 West 43rd St., New York, N. Y. 10036.
Buys short, topical light verse. Pays $3 per line. Also uses short compilations of humorous news items on a related topic.

THE NEW YORKER—25 West 43rd St., New York, N. Y. 10036.
Buys light verse, amusing bits printed in newspapers, books, magazines, etc., and entertaining anecdotes. Pays a minimum of $5, on acceptance; extra payment is made for titles and/or tag lines.

OCCUPATIONAL HAZARDS—812 Huron Rd., Cleveland, Ohio 44115.
Articles, from 500 words, on industrial safety, health, fire prevention, and security. Related cartoons and photos. Pays 2¢ a word and up, on publication, $3 for photos, $5 for cartoons, on acceptance.

OCEANOLOGY—Oceanology/Industrial Research, Inc., Beverly Shores, Ind. 46301.
Technical magazine on oceanography and related marine sciences. Uses some jokes and cartoons. Pays various rates, $5 per cartoon.

THE OHIO MOTORIST—2605 Euclid Ave., Cleveland, Ohio 44115.
Short humorous poems on motoring, automotive and vacation topics (foreign and domestic), preferably 4 or 6 lines. Pays $5.

OKLAHOMA RANCH AND FARM WORLD—Newspaper Printing Corp., 316 South Boulder, Tulsa, Okla.
Bimonthly Sunday supplement of the Tulsa *Sunday World*. Farm, suburban and homemaking fillers to ½ column. Pays $7.50 per column, on publication. Authors must query first.

ONE—422 South Fifth St., Minneapolis, Minn. 55415.
Lutheran. For older teen-agers. Uses some humorous verse. Pays 2¢ a word and up, on acceptance.

1,000 JOKES—750 Third Ave., New York, N. Y. 10017.
Buys funny verse, short humor, and novelty humor features. Does not buy jokes. Pays $5 for 4-line verse; $15 to $30 for short humor, 200 to 750 words; $15 to $50 for cartoons.

ORGANIC GARDENING AND FARMING—Emmaus, Pa.
Magazine devoted to aspects of organic agriculture. Pays $5 to $15 for fillers, on acceptance. Author's Handbook, Photographer's Guide and free copy sent on request.

THE ORPHAN'S MESSENGER—81 York St., Jersey City, N. J. 07302.
Catholic. Uses fillers and verse of 4 to 40 lines. Pays 1¢ to 3¢ a word, within a month.

OUR SUNDAY VISITOR—Huntington, Ind. 46750.
Catholic. Buys short material, under 250 words, for "People's Page." Also cartoons. Pays 10¢ a word and up for most material, $15 to $30 per cartoon, on acceptance.

OUTDOOR LIFE—355 Lexington Ave., New York, N. Y. 10017.
Buys short fact items and hints on hunting, fishing, camping, and the care and repair of firearms, fishing tackle, motor boats, and similar outdoor equipment. Pays on acceptance.

PARADE—733 Third Ave., New York, N. Y. 10017.
Sunday newspaper supplement. Short anecdotes, generally involving a well-known personality and telling an amusing and pointed story, for "Anecdote of the Week." Also buys text quizzes. Text quizzes should be informative and relate to real problems continually raised in the minds of readers. Payment on acceptance. Contact Richard Hubbard, Associate Editor.

PARENTS' MAGAZINE—52 Vanderbilt Ave., New York, N. Y. 10017.
For "Out of the Mouth of Babes," children's sayings. For "Family Clinic," uses short items on solution of some family problem: allowances, nap-taking, eating problems, etc. Pays $5 per item, on publication.

PEN—444 Sherman St., Denver, Colo. 80203.
Uses humorous or informative fillers, up to 200 words, of general interest. Pays 3¢ a word.

PENNSYLVANIA ANGLER—Pennsylvania Fish Commission, Harrisburg, Pa. 17120.
Some cartoons and fillers on fishing, boating, camping, etc., in Pennsylvania. Pays up to 3¢ a word.

PET FAIR—F.F.J. Enterprises, Inc., 527 Madison Ave., New York, N. Y. 10022.
Magazine for pet owners and animal lovers. Uses fillers, short humor,

jokes and puzzles, and verse for children or adults. Pays 5¢ a word and up.

PET LIFE—245 Cornelison Ave., Jersey City, N. J. 07302.
Jokes, anecdotes, riddles, animal quizzes, anagrams, etc., about pets and pet owners. Pays $2 for fillers.

PLAYBOY—HMH Publishing Co., Inc., 232 East Ohio St., Chicago, Ill. 60611.
High-quality entertainment magazine for urban men. Buys jokes for $25; "After Hours" items (brief amusing paragraphs on topical subjects) for $25 to $200. Address appropriate submissions to Party Jokes Editor or After Hours Editor.

POPULAR ELECTRONICS—One Park Ave., New York, N. Y. 10016.
Uses occasional electronics humor features. Pays $100 to $200, on acceptance.

POPULAR GARDENING AND LIVING OUTDOORS—383 Madison Ave., New York, N. Y. 10017.
Pays $5 for each acceptable "Garden Gimmick," an ingenious solution to a gardening problem, indoors or outdoors.

POPULAR MECHANICS MAGAZINE—575 Lexington Ave., New York, N. Y. 10022.
Buys short illustrated fact items and hints, 100 words and up, for "What's New for Your Home?" (new product) and "Shopping for Tools." Pays $12.50 and up per item, on acceptance. Also buys short articles with photos or drawings on new how-to ideas.

POPULAR PHOTOGRAPHY—One Park Ave., New York, N. Y. 10016.
Interested in material for "Photo Tips" and "Movie Tips" departments. Pays $10 for each illustrated "Tip." Payment is on acceptance.

POPULAR SCIENCE MONTHLY—355 Lexington Ave., New York, N. Y. 10017.
Short fact items and hints for special sections: "Hints from the Model Garage" (auto upkeep); "Short Cuts and Tips" (home shop hints and techniques); "I'd Like to See Them Make . . ." (pet ideas for gadgets readers would like to see in general use). If possible, glossy photos or rough sketches should accompany material. Pays $8 and up for shorts, on acceptance.

POULTRY TRIBUNE—Mt. Morris, Ill. 61054.
Stories from 200 words on egg production, processing, and marketing. Pays 2¢ to 5¢ a word, on acceptance.

PRO SHOP OPERATIONS—88 Scribner Ave., Norwalk, Conn. 06856.
Case histories of successful pro shop operations, and new ideas relating to merchandising, display, bookkeeping, etc., in a pro shop, 200 to 800 words, including short personal items on golf professionals. Pays on publication.

PROGRESS—Unity School of Christianity, Lee's Summit, Mo. 64063.
For young adults. Fillers, 100 to 500 words, on the application of
spiritual principles to everyday life. Also poetry, not over 16 lines.
Pays 2¢ a word for prose, 25¢ a line for poetry, on acceptance. Free
sample on request.

PROGRESSIVE GROCER—420 Lexington Ave., New York, N. Y.
10017.
Grocery merchandising publication. Humorous and inspirational fillers
and jokes, 300 words maximum. Pays $2 for jokes, more for fillers.

QUOTE—Droke House, Inc., P.O. Box 683, Anderson, S. C. 29622.
Uses material of value to public speakers: original humor to 100
words, 4-line light verse, quips, epigrams, jokes, and fillers. Material
must be original. Pays from $1, on publication.

RAMPARTS—301 Broadway, San Francisco, Calif.
Reviews of books, movies, plays, and any cultural event of national
interest; sideline and background news stories; satirical humor (no
anecdotes, light verse, jokes). Length: 1,500 to 2,000 words. "Mar-
ginalia" uses opinion and travel material to 1,500 words; "Ephemera"
uses material on art, cinema, and books, to 1,500 words. Pays 5¢ a
word, on publication.

RASCAL—See *The Men's Digest.*

READER'S DIGEST—Pleasantville, N. Y. 10570.
Buys contributions for "Life in These United States," "Humor in
Uniform," "Toward More Picturesque Speech," "Laughter, the Best
Medicine," "Quotable Quotes," "Personal Glimpses," "Campus
Comedy," etc. Contributors should watch magazine for announce-
ments of other departments. Address submissions to the Editor of each
department. Payment for previously unpublished anecdotes used in
"Life in These United States," "Campus Comedy," and "Humor in
Uniform" is $100, on publication. Payment for other original filler
items is $10 per *Digest* two-column line on publication. No fillers can
be acknowledged or returned.

REDBOOK MAGAZINE—230 Park Ave., New York, N. Y. 10017.
Wants informative or factual material of strong personal appeal or
importance to young married readers, 500 to 1,000 words. Uses verse
rarely. Payment on acceptance.

THE RHODE ISLANDER—Providence Sunday *Journal*, Providence,
R. I.
Sunday newspaper supplement. Uses short articles, not over 1,000
words, relating to Rhode Island, with photos. Pays up to $50, on
publication.

ROAD & TRACK—834 Production Pl., Newport Beach, Calif. 92663.
Magazine covering sports and imported cars, technical subjects, sports
car events. Uses amusing 1,000-word anecdotes. Payment varies.

ROD & GUN IN CANADA—1475 Metcalfe St., Montreal, Que., Canada.
Uses fillers with photos pertaining to hunting and fishing in Canada.
Pays 1½¢ to 2¢ a word, $2.50 to $5 per photo, on publication.

ROLL CALL: *The Newspaper of Capitol Hill*—324 C St., S.E., Washington, D. C. 20003.
Short, humorous items concerning Congress and Congressmen, anecdotes, puzzles, quips on political subjects. Payment on acceptance.

ROMP—See *Humorama, Inc.*

ROTARIAN—1600 Ridge Ave., Evanston, Ill.
Humorous articles of interest to business and professional men, to 1,200 words. Query first. Also uses 4-line original limericks for "Limerick Corner." Pays good rates for prose, $5 for limericks, on acceptance.

ST. JOSEPH MAGAZINE—St. Benedict, Ore. 97373.
Catholic. Special need for contributions to "The Best Sermon I Ever Heard" series, 800 to 1,800 words. Also humorous or light fiction, 1,000 to 4,000 words. Pays 2½¢ a word and up, on acceptance.

SAN FRANCISCO MAGAZINE—120 Green, San Francisco, Calif. 94111.
Uses short items pertaining to San Francisco, 10 to 100 words. Pays $10 to $25, on publication.

THE SATURDAY EVENING POST—641 Lexington Ave., New York, N. Y. 10022.
Limited market. No set requirements for editorial material. Most material staff-written or assigned through recognized literary agents. However, any finished manuscript addressed to the Post Scripts Editor will be read carefully.

SATURDAY REVIEW—380 Madison Ave., New York, N. Y. 10017.
Occasional brief articles (under 1,000 words) on the arts, other subjects covered by the magazine. Pays various rates. Also high-quality, humorous essays for the "Phoenix Nest." Authors should see column before submitting.

SCIENCE AND MECHANICS—505 Park Ave., New York, N. Y. 10022.
Buys shop hints for the home workshop, information on new tools, and general science news. Any length. Material should relate to everyday interests and concerns of average home craftsman. Payment varies, on acceptance.

SCIENCE DIGEST—1775 Broadway, New York, N. Y. 10019.
Science news monthly. Uses news items, up to 750 words, on important scientific, technological, and medical developments. Pays 5¢ to 10¢ a word, on acceptance.

SENIOR HI CHALLENGE—Church of God, 922 Montgomery Ave., Cleveland, Tenn. 37311.
Sunday School lesson and take-home paper. Verse, fillers, puzzles and

cartoons. Prayers and Scriptures for memorization for "Devotions" column. Length: 500 to 600 words. Pays ½¢ a word for short items, $1 for poems, $3 for cartoons, on acceptance.

SEVENTEEN—320 Park Ave., New York, N. Y. 10022.
Fashion and service magazine for teen-age girls. Short articles for "Face to Face" column; pays $100 to $150. Also buys photos and information for "Teen Scene." Payment varies, on acceptance.

SEVENTY-SIX MAGAZINE—P.O. Box 7600, Los Angeles, Calif. 90054.
Publication of the Union Oil Company of California. Uses some fillers if petroleum oriented. Pays on acceptance. Prefers author's query first.

SHOOTING TIMES—Box 1500, War Memorial Dr., Peoria, Ill.
Articles, from 250 words, on guns and pistols, hunting and shooting. Pays on acceptance. Query first.

SIGNATURE—*The Diner's Club Magazine*—10 Columbus Circle, New York, N. Y. 10019.
Humorous quotes. Pays on acceptance.

SKIING MAGAZINE—Ziff Davis Publishing Co., One Park Ave., New York, N. Y. 10016.
Humor and short articles, from 1,000 words, related to skiing. Query first. Pays from $100.

THE SKIPPER—2nd St. at Spa Creek, Annapolis, Md.
Boating magazine. Uses occasional light verse, about 2 to 10 lines, and cartoons. Payment is $5 and up, on acceptance.

SMALL WORLD—Volkswagen of America, Englewood Cliffs, N. J. 07632.
Quarterly. "Small Talk" column uses anecdotes about Volkswagen owners' experiences, cartoons, and photos about Volkswagens. Length: up to 100 words. Pays $10 minimum for short items, on acceptance.

SOUTHLAND MAGAZINE—Long Beach *Independent Press-Telegram,* Sixth and Pine, Long Beach, Calif. 90801.
Sunday newspaper supplement. Uses how-to and hobby fillers. Pays $5 to $10 per column, on publication.

SPORT MAGAZINE—205 East 42nd St., New York, N. Y. 10017.
For "Sportalk" column, wants sports notes, short items and anecdotes, from one paragraph to 1,000 words. Pays up to $25 for short items; to $75 for filler stories, on acceptance. Currently buying little free lance material.

SPORTFISHING—Yachting Publishing Corp., Room 600, 50 West 44th St., New York, N. Y. 10036.
Jokes and cartoons with a fishing emphasis. Pays on acceptance.

SPORTS AFIELD—959 Eighth Ave., New York, N. Y. 10019.
Fillers on hunting, fishing, camping, boating, shooting, 100 to 700 words. Photographs are almost a must. Unusual and useful gimmicks

and tips for sportsmen are the most acceptable. Rates up to $100, on acceptance.

SPORTS CAR GRAPHIC—5959 Hollywood Blvd., Los Angeles, Calif. 90028.
Humor and technically accurate cartoons with sports car or road racing slant. Pays on acceptance. Query first.

SPORTS ILLUSTRATED—Rockefeller Center, New York, N. Y. 10020.
Buys short, off-the-news features from 600 words, humor, reminiscences. Pays $250 for short features, on acceptance.

STORYTIME—Baptist Sunday School Board, 127 Ninth Ave. North, Nashville, Tenn. 37203.
For children 4 to 8. Uses occasional short how-to articles (100 to 300 words) on things children can make, simple quizzes, and verse to 12 lines. Pays on acceptance.

SUCCESSFUL FARMING—1716 Locust St., Des Moines, Iowa.
Buys light verse, hints, recipes, quips and jokes. Special departments: "Successful Recipes," "All Around the House" (hints), "All Around the Farm" (hints), and "Tips for the Cook" (hints). Pays $3 to $5, on acceptance, for jokes and newsbreaks for the "Laughing at Life" humor column. Newsbreaks must be actual tear sheets, including name of paper. Other payment on publication. Material cannot be returned.

SUNDAY DIGEST—850 North Grove Ave., Elgin, Ill. 60120.
Weekly Protestant publication for older youth and adults. Original anecdotes to 500 words, inspirational or humorous. Pays $2 to $15. Timely vignettes, quizzes, quotations for "Sunday Scrapbook," to 300 words. Seasonal and holiday material must be submitted ten to twelve months in advance. Pays up to $10. Short, pithy, original epigrams pinpointing Christian virtues or frailties for "Thought Stretchers." Pays $2.50 to $5. All payment is on acceptance. Material will be returned if stamped, self-addressed envelope is enclosed.

SUNDAY SCHOOL LIFE—American Sunday-School Union, 1816 Chestnut St., Philadelphia, Pa. 19103.
Sunday School periodical. Biblical puzzles, anecdotes with Christian application, short fact items (also with Christian application), letters relating to missionary endeavor, Sunday School work or incidents, 500 to 1,000 words. Pays on acceptance.

SUNSET—Lane Publishing Co., Menlo Park, Calif.
Monthly western "how-to-do-it" magazine. Buys good *ideas* only for the home (no manuscripts purchased) and recipes. Pays $5 to $15 for ideas, $5 to $25 for recipes, on publication. Accepts material only from persons living in magazine's circulation area (Hawaii, California, Idaho, Nevada, Washington, Oregon, Arizona, and Utah).

SURFER MAGAZINE—Box 1028, Dana Point, Calif. 92629.
Surfing magazine. Humor, humorous poems, cartoons, news items. Must relate to surfing. "Pipeline" uses news items and photos. Length:

under 200 words. Pays $5 for "Pipeline" items and photos, on publication.

TV GUIDE—Radnor, Pa. 19088.
Short humor pertaining to television for one-page "TV Jibe" feature. Items must fit on one *TV Guide* page or may be shorter. Payment varies.

TEEN SCREEN—6425 Hollywood Blvd., Hollywood, Calif. 90028.
Fan-oriented teen magazine. Uses star poems from teens only, up to 150 words. Pays on acceptance.

TEEN TIME—Light and Life Press, Winona Lake, Ind. 46590.
Sunday School take-home paper. Uses some verse. Pays 20¢ a line, on acceptance.

TELEFLORA'S SPIRIT—900 North Sepulveda, El Segundo, Calif. 90245.
For retail florists, subscribers to Teleflora's services (flowers by wire). Short humor pieces, 500 to 1,000 words, dealing with some aspect of retail floristry. Pays $20, on acceptance.

THIS DAY—3558 South Jefferson, St. Louis, Mo. 63118.
Christian family magazine. Uses occasional light or serious verse. Payment is on acceptance.

THIS WEEK—485 Lexington Ave., New York, N. Y. 10017.
Short pieces for "People in Action" (personalities) and "Idea Exchange" (self-help) features. Pays $35 to $50 for "People in Action" and $10 to $20 for "Idea Exchange."

TODAY—Harvest Publications, 5750 North Ashland Ave., Chicago, Ill. 60626.
Evangelical Christian magazine for adults. Buys 400-word anecdotes and 400-word how-to-do-it and advice articles. Pays 2¢ a word and up, on acceptance. Query first. Information packet on this and other papers, 50¢.

TODAY'S FAMILY—Onamia, Minn. 56359.
Catholic family magazine. Fillers of 250 words. Pays 2¢ to 5¢, on acceptance.

TOGETHER—Box 423, Park Ridge, Ill.
For Methodist families. Uses true personal incidents, short humor, and short verse. "Getting Along Together" pays $5 for short, true anecdotes about events which "brightened a day or lightened a heart." Payment for other items varies.

TRAILER LIFE—10148 Riverside Dr., Toluca Lake, North Hollywood, Calif. 91602.
Material on trailering and related interests. Illustrated "how-to" articles to 800 words; travel pieces 100 to 125 words. Pays $15 to $50, on publication. Write for Editor's Guide. Same address and requirements for *Travel Trailer News*.

TRAILERING GUIDE—Rajo Publications, Inc., 215 Park Ave. South, New York, N. Y. 10003.
For owners of travel trailers, pick-up truck campers, and motor homes. Cartoons. Pays $10, on publication.

TRAVEL TRAILER NEWS—See *Trailer Life.*

TREASURE—American Sunday-School Union, 1816 Chestnut St., Philadelphia, Pa. 19103.
For children 8 to 12. Uses some puzzles, quizzes, and how-to-do articles, no more than 500 words, with a definite Biblical and spiritual slant. Payment varies.

TREASURE HUNTER'S GUIDE—P.O. Drawer L, Conroe, Tex. 77301.
Quarterly magazine about lost mines, buried or sunken treasure. Uses short "Treasure Nuggets," 300 to 500 words. Pays $5 for fillers, on acceptance.

TRUE—67 West 44th St., New York, N. Y. 10036.
Adventure magazine for men. Buys fillers about adventure, sports, travel, humor, etc. Pays good rates. Query before submitting material.

TRUE ACTION—See *Male.*

TRUE CONFESSIONS—205 East 42nd St., New York, N. Y. 10017.
Buys a limited number of seriously-handled self-help and inspirational fillers, 300 to 800 words, using "you" approach. Home-making material is handled by staff. Pays 5¢ a word, on acceptance.

TRUE EXPERIENCE—205 East 42nd St., New York, N. Y. 10017.
Fillers up to 150 words, for "Most Embarrassing Experience," "Out of the Mouths of Babes," "Child's Drawing," "Lucky Story," "Laughs," "Pet Animal Crackers," "Hints to New Mothers," and "The Experience That Changed My Life." Payment is $5 to $10.

TRUE ROMANCE—205 East 42nd St., New York, N. Y. 10017.
Pays $10 for short personal-experience items for columns: "Laugh in Your Life," "Pet Peeves," "Family Album"; also same rates for photos submitted for "Kid Stuff" and "Your Pets" columns. Pays $10 to $25 for cartoon captions matching cartoon of the month in "Tag the Gag" contest.

TRUE WEST—P.O. Box 3668, Austin, Tex. 78704.
Uses short factual items about the West, 500 to 900 words. Please cite sources. Photos helpful, originals returned after publication. Pays 1¢ a word minimum. Same address and requirements for *Frontier Times.*

U. S. LADY—620 Warner Bldg., Washington, D. C. 20004.
Humorous verse, 2 to 20 lines, pertaining to military and Foreign Service life; true, humorous anecdotes of military and overseas living, of interest to wives of U. S. service men and Foreign Service personnel. Pays $2 per item.

THE UPPER ROOM—1908 Grand Ave., Nashville, Tenn. 37203.
Meditations on Bible texts, 250 words, with illustrations. Pays $3, on publication. Leaflet on writing meditations and list of topics sent on request.

UPWARD—Baptist Sunday School Board, 127 Ninth Ave. North, Nashville, Tenn. 37203.
For Southern Baptist Youth 13 to 17. Puzzles and quizzes, poetry to 16 lines. Pays 2¢ a word, on acceptance.

VISION—Christian Board of Publication, P.O. Box 179, St. Louis, Mo. 63166.
For young people 12 to 18. Uses a few cartoons, short humorous pieces, puzzles, humorous poems. Pays 1¢ a word and up for prose, about 25¢ a line for poetry, $5 and up for cartoons and puzzles.

WESTART—Box 428, Auburn, Calif.
Artists' newspaper. Primarily concerned with current news items in the arts field. Uses short features, 350 to 500 words, of exceptional interest in the field of crafts and fine arts. No hobbies. Pays 20¢ per column inch, on publication.

WOMAN'S DAY—67 West 44th St., New York, N. Y. 10036.
Uses fillers about human experiences, home topics, party ideas, and crafts. Also buys short humor. No verse. Best length is about 500 words. Payment varies and is on acceptance. "Neighbors" column pays $10 for each letter and $5 for each brief, practical suggestion. Address "Neighbors" items to Martha V. Reynolds, Neighbor Editor.

WORDS OF CHEER—Mennonite Publishing House, Scottdale, Pa.
Children's story paper. Light verse to 24 lines, puzzles, quizzes, some cartoons, human interest photos with brief explanations. Pays $3 and up for puzzles and quizzes, 25¢ a line for verse, $5 to $10 for photo features. Sample copies available on request.

THE WORKBASKET—4251 Pennsylvania, Kansas City, Mo. 64111.
Monthly needlework magazine. For "Women Who Make Cents" column, short items of 200 words or less about how a woman adds to the family income. Pays 2¢ a word, on acceptance.

YANKEE MAGAZINE—Dublin, N. H.
Monthly magazine about New England. Uses unusual one-page articles, around 500 words, on any subject relating to New England. Photos wanted if possible. "Small Business & Crafts" column uses items under 400 words about New England's small businesses and/or hobbies. Payment is $10 for "Small Business & Crafts" items, if written by someone other than the subject or his family. Pays $25 to $200 for articles and fiction; $7.50 to $10 for photos, on publication.

THE YOUNG JUDAEAN—116 West 14th St., New York, N. Y.
Humor about modern Israel, contemporary American Jewish child life, filler-anecdotes, short poems for important Zionist events and

personalities of interest to Jewish children, 8 to 13 years old. Pays $5 to $15.

YOUNG MISS (formerly *Calling All Girls*)—52 Vanderbilt Ave., New York, N. Y. 10017.
Magazine for young teen-agers. Wants how-to hints for teen-agers, especially clever things to make out of odds and ends, up to 100 words. Pays $5 per item, on acceptance.

YOUR NEW BABY—Parents' Magazine Enterprises, Inc., 52 Vanderbilt Ave., New York, N. Y. 10017.
Specialty magazine for new and expectant mothers. Uses fillers of 300 to 500 words; anecdotes, humor, light verse, hints of varying lengths. Pays $15 to $75, on acceptance.

YOUTH IN ACTION—Free Methodist Youth, Winona Lake, Ind. 46590.
For 17- to 18-year-old readers. Uses some fillers, short humor, jokes, puzzles, and some short verse. Pays 1¢ a word for prose, 10¢ a line for poetry, on acceptance.

ZEST—*The Houston Chronicle,* 512-20 Travis St., Houston, Tex. 77002. Don Warren, *Zest* Editor.
Sunday newspaper supplement. Short, humorous articles of general interest. Pays $10 to $20, after publication.

ZIP—See *Humorama, Inc.*